MW00713320

풍성한 복음 선교회
Abundant Gospel Mission
P.O. Box 851272
Richardson, Tx 75085

THE GOSPEL FOR
SALVATION

PAUL I. SHIN

Translated by Hayeon Kim

CROSSBOOKS
PUBLISHING

CrossBooks™
A Division of LifeWay
1663 Liberty Drive
Bloomington, IN 47403
www.crossbooks.com
Phone: 1-866-879-0502

First published by CrossBooks 05/01/2014

ISBN: 978-1-4627-3593-8 (sc)
ISBN: 978-1-4627-3594-5 (e)

Printed in the United States of America.

This book is printed on acid-free paper.

CONTENTS

PREFACE

was born into a Christian family. My father was a church elder, but up until I turned 30 years old, I had not known about salvation; I was just attending a Christian church. In my freshman and sophomore years at college, I began to ask myself, "Why are there evil people if God is alive?"

I doubted the existence of God. But while I was living as an immigrant in the U.S.A, I finally experienced salvation. During my ministry, I have met a lot of people who were just like me. As a result, I asked God to lead me in how to teach these people so that they can come to know salvation. This book is a guide to help people to understand how a sinner can be saved by God and how to live as a Christian.

We often hear the words "Gospel" and "The Good News". The Bible says in Mark 1:15 that we have to believe the Good News—the Gospel—in order to be saved. Through Romans 10:9-10, we learn that there are three important things about the Good News and that there are two ways to believe the Good News.

The Bible says that without knowing these truths, we cannot be saved. The beginning of faith is salvation; therefore, it is not an option but is mandatory. And we should preach this to the ones who have yet to come into this knowledge.

This book is written in Korean with translations available in Japanese, Spanish, Chinese, Russian, Pakistani and English and is being read and used by many. I pray that this book will be helpful for your Christian life.

PART 1.
INTRODUCTION

And you also were included in Christ when you heard the word of truth, the Gospel of your salvation. Having believed, you were marked in him with a seal, the promised Holy Spirit.
Ephesians 1:13

SALVATION BY FAITH

In the first book of textbook for newcomers and newly converted Christians (*Seven Steps*, published by Baltimore Bethel Church), which has been used for our church, Korean World Mission Baptist Church, we ask three important fundamental life questions.

1. Where do I come from?
2. Why do I live in this world?
3. Where am I really heading to?

These questions have been at the forefront of debate between eastern and western philosophers from long ago. Even modern philosophers are still seeking the answers to these questions. To be frank, this shows us that the human race has not yet found a clear answer to these questions. But the Bible, the Word of God, gives us clear answers.

Evolutionists, who do not believe in the creation of all things by God, say that man is a highly evolved ape-like creature, evolved from a microorganism. But this notion is just a theory and not proven science, although it's been treated as science and taught to children in school. But no one has been able to provide evidence in support of this theory.

The Bible clearly says that it is God who created all the animals, birds, fish and creeping things according to their kinds (Genesis 1:21, 25). And according to His image, He created man (Genesis 1:27). The world was not created through evolution, but by God. In other words, it came from God. Because of the Bible, we also know and believe that Adam and Eve, the first human beings, were created by God.

WHERE DO I COME FROM?

The first question in the first book is "Where do I come from?" Generally, people say that they came through and from their parents. But the Bible says that not only Adam and Eve, but all mankind come from the Lord. Even I, who am living in the 21st century, came from the Lord. If this is true, can we provide any evidence? The Bible gives us this proof:

> *Know that the LORD is God. It is He who **made** us,*
> *and we are his: we are his people, the sheep of his pasture.*
> *Psalm 100:3*

2층 우리를 게으성미요 ⁓

Psalm 100 was written about 1,000 before Christ came to this earth. The writer uses the words "we" and "us" to confess that all men were created by God.

> Yet, O LORD, you are our Father. We are the clay, you are the potter: we are **all the work of your hand.**
>
> Isaiah 64:8

A prophet named Isaiah, moved by the Spirit of God, wrote Isaiah 64 about 700 years before the birth of Christ. Even he uses the terms "we" and "us" to declare that all man is created by and comes from the Lord.

If those people who were living on this earth 1,000 years ago and those who were living 700 years ago were creations of God, are we not? We certainly are creations of God—not only Adam and Eve, but also all men and women are creations made by the hands of God.

After Adam and Eve, God created men and women through their parents. The Bible says that God created us in "the mother's womb."

> For you **created** my inmost being: you **knit me** together in my mother's womb.
>
> Psalm 139: 13

> This is what the LORD says--he who **made you,** who **formed you in the womb,** and who will help you
>
> Isaiah 44:2

> Did not he who **made me in the womb** make them? Did not the same one **form us** both within our mothers?
>
> Job 31:15

3

God created and knitted us in our mothers' womb. These words tell us that it is God who makes a child through his parents, not that children are made and born naturally. No parents can say, "I made my child's arm" or "I made my child's head." God made the child through his parents.

Knit means that God has put every part of the body together. A man and a woman marry, and a child is born between them, but it is not they who make the child; it is God who creates and knits the child in the mother's womb.

The Bible also tells us the steps through which God created us:

> *Did you not pour me out like **milk** and **curdle** me like cheese* 주께서 나를 젖과 같이 쏟으셨으며 *Job 10:10*

Job says God has poured him out as milk and curdled him like cheese in his mother's womb. He does not say that it was his father, but that it was God who did these things. It is not easy to understand what Job is saying, but these words show us how God creates us.

I was not able to understand the part "my father begat me (Jeremiah 16:3) and my mother raised me" from the famous Korean poetry by Chul Chung. To me, it seemed that the mother begets a child, not the father. I have never seen a father bear and raise a child. I was able to understand this finally after a middle school biology class. It might be hard for you to understand this, too. But I am sure that you will understand it sooner or later. The Bible says that God curdled the milk like cheese.

What happens then?

*Clothe me with **skin** and **flesh** and knit me together
with **bones** and sinews.*

파우와 살을 내게 입히시며
뼈와 힘줄로 나를 엮으셨으므 . *Job 10:11*

Then, God clothes with skin and flesh and knits together
with bones and sinews. All this is done by God, not by our
parents. We use the term "natural science" to imply that these
things happen naturally, apart from God, but there is nothing
that comes naturally in this sense. Whether Christian or not,
all men are created by God and exist because of His creation.
A human has approximately 206 bones, and none of those
bones are made by his parents; it all comes from the Lord. I
want to point out what else the Bible says about this:

*You gave me **life** and showed me **kindness**, and in
your providence watched over my **spirit**.*

생명과 은혜를 내게 주시고 *Job 10:12*

God gives those He creates life and spirit. Animals,
birds and fish have life but no spirit. God only breathed the
breath of life into man (Genesis 2:7). We are spiritual beings.
So even when our lives on this earth end, our spirits will
continue to live in heaven or hell. That God showed him
kindness means that Job was able to survive the water of his
mother's womb and that this was a grace from the Lord.

*Why then did you bring me out of **the womb**?*

주께서 나를 태에서 나오게 *Job 10:18*
하셨은

It is the Lord, our Father, who brings the baby out of the
womb of his mother. Neither a mother nor father is able to
decide the time that a baby will be born. God brings the baby
out of the mother's womb according to His time.

As I have mentioned, it is God who creates us in the mother's womb, who knits us and brings us out of our mother's womb. So "we all come from the Lord, our heavenly Father."

We say generally that it is the farmer who farms. It is not wrong to say that. But let's think about it. The farmer sows seeds, weeds a field, and harvests. But it is God who makes the seed sprout, grow, bloom, make fruits, and ripen (Psalm 65:9-13; Isaiah 28:23-29). Then who is the one who farms? Is it the farmer? Or is it God? The farmer makes efforts and works hard, but it is the Lord, God, who farms.

There may be some who will then ask, "How is God the one who farms? It all happens naturally." They say that plants grow according to nature, if the light, water, and soil are in good condition. But who gave us the light? Who gave the soil and the water? It was not made by the farmer, but it was formed by God. God created the land, supplies the air, gives the rain, gives the light, and gives the seasons (Genesis 1:1; Matthew 5:45). But scientists do not want to believe this and, instead, use the term "natural science."

It is God who forms us and our parents who, in pain, bear us and have to make the efforts. God gave us a commandment to obey and honor our parents who do all that for us (Exodus 20:12, 21:17; Leviticus 19:3). Therefore, we should obey and honor our parents (Ephesians 6:1-3)

Now the rising question should be, "What about the children who are born with physical, mental and ethical disabilities? Are they born like that by a mistake of God?" The Bible says that these maladies are not caused by God but by the schemes of man.

> *This only have I found: God **made mankind upright**,*
> *but men have gone in search of many **schemes**.*
> 하나님은 사람을 정직하게 지으셨으나 *Ecclesiastes 7:29*
> 사람이 많은 꾀들을 낸 것이니라 꺼

Even the king of wisdom, King Solomon, posed the question, "How can a baby be born with physical, mental or ethical disabilities?" And in his old age, he came to realize that these things occur not by the hand of God, but by the schemes of man.

God made mankind physically, mentally and ethically upright. But after sin entered the world, humans, who sinned, have followed their own schemes, which cause children to be born with disabilities. Let's have a look at the Bible for an example:

> *Has not the LORD made them one? In flesh and*
> *spirit they are his. And why one? Because he was*
> *seeking **godly offspring**.*
> 경건한 자손을 얻고자 *Malachi 2:15*

God created Eve for Adam, even though He could have created more men and women; He created only Adam for Eve. He did this because He was seeking godly offspring. These words mean that if a man ignores the will of God and is sexually involved with many different women (or a woman does the same with many different men), he cannot have godly offspring. A man being intimate with anyone other than his wife is nothing but a scheme—a sin against God. The consequences of this sin might appear in the next generation or later and may include physical, mental and ethical disabilities in future children.

These things are caused by man, who pollutes the water, air and environment, not by God. God never makes mistakes.

WHY AM I LIVING IN THIS WORLD?

The second question in the first book of 'Seven Steps' is "Why am I living in this world?" The answer to this question is "to find a way back to the Lord, our God." At the beginning, we discuss the fact that we actually come from the Lord. Because we are from the Lord, we will one day have to return to heaven with God or to the hell with the devil. But the problem is that we cannot see "the way" (Ecclesiastes 12:7). We do not know where to and how to return to that way. Many people have sought the way back to where we came from, but no one has been able to find it. But our Lord Jesus, who came to the earth 2,000 years ago, explains it in the following way:

> Jesus answered, "I am the **way** and the truth and the life. No one comes to the Father except through me. 내 가 곧 길이요 진리요 생명 John 14:6

Jesus says that He is the only way to the Father, and this is true; He is the only way. Only through Jesus can we go to the Father and to heaven.

As we are born to our parents, we are already heading to hell because of our sins. We are not given a choice. But because of Jesus, we can choose to go to heaven or hell. If this is true, how can we meet Jesus who came 2,000 years ago, and how can we go to heaven?

> Then choose for yourselves this day whom you will serve 나-와 내 집은 여호와를 섬기겠 Joshua 24:15

There are only two choices: one is heaven, and the other is hell. There is no in between and no other place for taking a rest. Someday in our lives, we all will have to die; there will be some of us resting in peace with God, but the others will suffer pain in hell.

Therefore, we have to find a way to God the Father. The Bible says that there is a way that seems right to a man, but in the end it leads to death (Proverbs 14:12, 16:25). You might think that you are the wisest man in the world and that you have been choosing the right way all along, but if you haven't met Jesus yet, your life is nothing but a foolish and failed one (Luke 16:23). You have to know this truth. Finding a way to the Father—to heaven—is the most important thing in your life. Do not hesitate as though it does not apply to you. Jesus said that He is the way to the Father, so make a choice while you can. All man should seek the way and go through that way while they can.

There are many serious and important matters in our lives, like marriage, education, careers and so on. But finding the way to the Father, our God, is more important and serious than any of these things (Deuteronomy 30:15-20; Hosea 6:1; Amos 4:6; Acts 9:35, 14:15).

WHERE AM I HEADING?

Which path have you been walking on? If you do not know where you are heading to by now, you must be heading to hell. The destination of your way is hell, where you will suffer and from which you will never be able to escape (Mathew 25:41). Your parents cannot lead you to the Father; no one but Jesus can.

Way can either be interpreted literally, as "the way" or "the method." In other words, Jesus can be the way and the method by which to go to the Father. The Bible says that the method is believing in Jesus. But this is not easy to understand. What does believing in Jesus mean? How can we believe in Jesus and go to heaven through Him?

There are three ways that we must <u>believe in Jesus</u> (Romans 10:9). Let's read the following verse:

> That if you confess with your mouth, "Jesus is **Lord**," and believe in your heart that God **raised** him from **the dead**, you **will be saved**.
>
> 내가 믿을 때 믿음   *Romans 10:9*
> 예수를 주로 시인하기

This passage describes well how we can come to salvation by following these three things:

1. Confess with our mouth, "Jesus is Lord."
2. Believe that He has paid the debt for our sins by His death on the cross.
3. Believe that He rose again from the dead.

There are many people—even Christians—who do not know how to explain these things when they are asked. There are even people who say that only believing in Jesus' death on the cross and His resurrection will bring one salvation. But they have misunderstood what the words of 1 Corinthians 15:1-4. In this chapter, the writer tells us about the resurrection. To tell us about the resurrection, the writer talks about the death first, then about the resurrection. But this is just a part of the Gospel, not the whole.

Verses 3-4 say that Jesus died for our sins and that he was buried and raised on the third day, according to the Scriptures. So people who hold this theory based on 1 Corinthians 15:1-4 say that confessing that Jesus is our Lord is merely something we need to be sanctified after we have salvation by believing in the death of Christ on the cross and in His resurrection. But they have misunderstood part of the Scriptures. According to their theory, Romans 10:9 cannot be explained. We have to pay attention to the all the words of Scripture, and Romans 10:9 says that we not only have to believe Christ's death and resurrection, but also confess that Jesus is our Lord in order to be saved.

After he was filled with the Holy Spirit on the day of Pentecost, Peter stood up and preached for the first time that God had made this Jesus, whom the people crucified, both Lord and Christ.

> *God has made this **Jesus**, whom you crucified, both **Lord** and **Christ**.*
>
> Acts 2:36

너희가 십자가에 못 박은
이 예수를 하나님이 주와 그리스도가 되게 하셨느니라

The Bible says that "more and more men and women believed in the Lord and were added to their number" (Acts 5:14). It also says, "The God of our fathers raised Jesus from the dead--whom you had killed by hanging him on a tree. [31] God exalted him to his own right hand as Prince and Savior that he might give repentance and forgiveness of sins to Israel" (Acts 5:30-31). In Acts, we can trace how the disciples taught the Jerusalem church about Jesus who came as the Lord and King. As a result of their teaching, many people turned to the Lord (Acts 9:35), and many believed in the Lord (Acts 9:42).

Peter taught that Jesus is Lord everywhere he went, and those who heard his teachings turned to the Lord and believed; that's how they were able to have faith in the Lord Jesus. But unfortunately, many churches in Korea have not begun their teaching with the truth that Jesus is Lord. As a result, many people live two contradictory lives: as Christians while in church and unbelievers while outside of the church. Because of this, Korean churches have been criticized by society.

The first thing, Peter preached to Cornelius was the truth that Jesus is Lord and the Christ.

> ...*Telling the good news of peace through Jesus Christ, who is* **Lord** *of all.*
> 1관유의 주 화전. 예두X
>
> Acts 10:36

The first people who preached the good news to the people in Antioch preached the same truth—that Jesus is Lord and the Christ.

> *Men from Cyprus and Cyrene, went to Antioch and began to speak to Greeks also, telling them the good news about* **the Lord** *Jesus.* **The Lord's** *hand was with them, and a great number of people believed and turned to* **the Lord.**
> 주의 손이 그들과
> 한꼐 하시매
>
> Acts 11:20-21

Barnabas went to Antioch and preached and encouraged all people "to remain true to the Lord with all their hearts" (Acts 11:23). These people—the disciples—were the first to be called Christians at Antioch as a result of this. From the outset churches should thoroughly teach that Jesus is the Lord in order to make true Christians. The apostle Paul also thoroughly taught people that Jesus is Lord on his first, second, and third mission trips.

> ...*They told how the Gentiles had been converted. This news made all the brothers very glad.*
> 주께 돌아온 잃은 막하여
> 다 주께 기뻐하니라
>
> Acts 15:3

This is what happened, as Paul reported to churches in Phoenicia and Samaria while he was on the way to Jerusalem after his first mission trip.

The apostle Paul wrote letters from Macedonia to the churches in Corinth when he was on his third mission trip. He wrote that he taught Jesus as Lord on his second mission trip.

> *For we do not preach ourselves, but Jesus Christ as Lord, and ourselves as your servants for Jesus' sake.*
>
> 예수를 전파 ⌐   2 Corinthians 4:5

We can see what Paul did on his third mission trip from Colossians 2:6. He wrote "So then, just as you received Christ Jesus As Lord." Not only Romans 10:9, but the whole New Testament says that we will have salvation by confessing that Jesus is Lord and by believing in the death and resurrection of Christ. Ever since the early churches, confessing Jesus as Lord has been important part. Let us take a look at what Jesus said:

> *Now this is eternal life: that they may **know** you, the only true God, and Jesus Christ, whom you have sent.*
>
> 영생은 예수X를 아는것 ⌐ John 17:3

It would have been easier for us to understand if he had said that eternal life is believing in Jesus. But he said that eternal life is that we may know him.(Col 1:10; 2Pet 1:2) This verse tells us that we cannot have salvation and eternal life unless we know God and Jesus.

Even in the Old Testament, God says, "Let us acknowledge the Lord: let us press on to acknowledge him" (Hosea 6:3). Israelites were chosen people, but because they lacked knowledge of Him, they were destroyed. "My people are destroyed from lack of knowledge" (Hosea 4:6).

> *The man who says, "I know him, but does not do what*
> *he commands is a liar, and the truth is not in him.* 1 John 2:4

2를 아느라하고 그의 계명을
지키지 아니하는 자는 거짓말

Knowing Jesus means that you know who He is, that you believe Him, and that you do what He commands. Even if you know and believe Him, if you do not follow his command to love one another, but instead have envy and selfish ambition, you do not have true faith (James 3:14-16).

Even though the Israelites were chosen people, they committed sin against God by worshipping idols because of their lack of knowledge of Him. Not only that, but they also leaned on those who captured them in Babylon instead of on God.

Even then, they weren't able to understand why God allowed them to be taken captive in Babylon. For them, they were chosen people. But throughout Ezekiel (chapters 6-39), God says more than 60 times, "You will know that I am the Lord." God says this repeatedly because He wants to let them know that they were destroyed by their lack of knowledge of Him.

For the Israelites, it was more important to know Him than to bring any offerings to Him (Isaiah 1:11). What did God say to Israelites through the prophet Jeremiah? "I will give them a heart to know me, that I am the Lord. They will be my people, and I will be their God, for they will return to me with all their heart" (Jeremiah 24:7). Without knowing God and Jesus, you cannot have true faith.

> *For I desire mercy, not sacrifice, and **acknowledgment** *
> ***of God** rather than burnt offerings.*
>
> 나는 인애를 원하고 제사를 원하지
> 아니하며 번제보다 하나님을 아는것을 원하노라 *Hosea 6:6*

Some biblical scholars say that the burnt offering symbolizes sacrifice, and we acknowledge a sacrifice to God as mature faith. But the Bible says that knowing the Lord, God, is much more precious than any sacrifice. It is not possible for one to have mature faith unless one knows God.

In New Testament times, it was said that there is no eternal life without knowing the true God and Jesus Christ, whom God has sent (John 17:3). Think about what the apostle Paul said after he met Jesus:

> *But whatever was to my profit I now consider loss for the sake of Christ. What is more, I consider everything a loss compared to **the surpassing greatness of knowing Christ Jesus my Lord**, for whose sake I have lost all things. I consider them rubbish, that I may gain Christ and be found in him, not having a righteousness of my own that comes from the law, but that which is through faith in Christ--the righteousness that comes from God and is by faith.*
>
> 예수를 아는 지식이 가장 고귀하기 *Philippians 3:7-9*

The apostle Paul was an intellectual, well-educated person who was born into a good family. He was able to have social success, but after he met Jesus, his only confession was this: that he considered everything a loss compared to the surpassing greatness of knowing Christ Jesus. Not only that, he said that he considered them to be rubbish. If you still don't know Jesus deeply and are still unable to have a personal relationship and fellowship with Him, then you either have a faith that still needs to grow, or you have a problem.

If you want to know more about Jesus, read the four Gospels of the New Testament, for these books tell you who He is:

Matthew 1-26: about who Jesus is
Matthew 27: about His death
Matthew 28: about the resurrection of Christ
Mark 1-14: about who Jesus is
Mark 15: about His death
Mark 16: about the resurrection
Luke 1-22: about who Jesus is
Luke 23: about the death of Christ
Luke 24: about the resurrection
John 1-18: about who Jesus is
John 19: about the death of Christ
John 20: about the resurrection of Christ
John 21: about after the resurrection

All four Gospels emphasize who Jesus is more than His death or the resurrection. This shows us how important it is to know Him. Matthew, Mark and Luke recorded almost the same content about who Jesus is (which makes up about 70% of each book), because it is so important to know Jesus. In the book of John, there are seven verses that begin with "I am." This is what God says in the Old Testament to show who He is. In the same way, this phrase is recorded seven times in John to tell people who Jesus is.

Pascal said, "Knowing Jesus will let you know the purpose of all things." In other words, if you do not know Jesus, you can't know the things in heaven or on earth. The truth is that you cannot know eternal life or anything else unless you know Jesus. Solomon said that everything is meaningless—a chasing after the wind (Ecclesiastes 1:14)—if one does not know God (Jesus). The Bible says this about the people who do not know God or have belief in Him:

> 🖎 *Therefore they will be like the morning mist, like the early dew that disappears, like chaff swirling from a threshing floor, like smoke escaping through a window.* Hosea 13:3

The book of Romans explains salvation well. But even though it explains salvation well, this book is not known as a Gospel. Matthew, Mark, Luke and John are the four Gospels because these books contain the Gospel. The Book of Romans tells us how we can respond to the Gospel and have faith by the Gospel to have salvation and be righteous. The four Gospels mostly tell us who Jesus is. They also tell us about Christ's death as redemption and about the resurrection.

To have eternal life, you must first know who Jesus is: He lived as a carpenter in Nazareth (Mark 6:3); He turned water into wine (John 2:9); even demons (Luke 8:28), a strong wind, and rough waters obeyed His words (Mark 4:39); and He fed 5,000 men with five barley loaves and two fish and "filled twelve baskets with the pieces of the five barley loaves left over by those who had eaten" (John 6:13).

Jesus asked His disciples, "Who do people say I am?" and after three years of training, He asked them, "Who do you say I am?" (Mark 16:15; Matthew 8:29; Luke 9:20; and John 9:17). This is the main point of the Gospel—the one thing one should know first as a Christian. To this question, Peter answered, "You are the Christ, the son of the living God" (Matthew 16:16). This confession of Peter says that Jesus is the Christ and the Son of the living God. And this is what I want to talk about. After Jesus heard Peter's confession, from that time on, Jesus began to explain that He must go to Jerusalem and suffer many things and that he must be killed and, on the third day, be raised to life (Matthew 16:21; Mark 8:31; Luke 9:22).

Before Peter's confession, Jesus had never mentioned his death or that he had to suffer and be resurrected. This demonstrates that it is not even worth talking about the death or the resurrection of the Christ unless one first knows who Jesus is. The death of Christ and His resurrection will have no meaning unless one knows who Jesus is.

Jesus is the King of Kings (Matthew), but He lived as a servant (Mark). He was a human (Luke), but also a perfect God (John). Confessing that Jesus is the Christ and the Lord is of first importance. Even if you believe in the death and the resurrection of Christ, but haven't confessed that Jesus is your Lord, you may not have salvation yet (Romans 10:9).

HOW CAN WE BELIEVE IN JESUS?

Now let's look at the Word of God to find out how we can come to faith.

> For it is with your **heart** that you **believe** and are justified, and it is with **your mouth** that you **confess** and are saved.
>
> 마음으로 믿어
> 입으로 시인
> *Romans 10:10*

Romans 10:10 tells us how we can come to faith:

1. We have to believe (three things of faith) in our hearts.
2. We have to confess (three things of faith) with our mouths.

We say that we will have eternal life and forgiveness of our sins by having faith in the Lord Jesus, and that is something we all know. But many people do not know what faith is and how to have it.

There are three things about faith that provide the basics of what it means to be a Christian. If you do not know these things, your faith and Christian life will not grow. Those who do not know these things will not be able to experience peace and joy in their lives. They will be Christians in name only, not having any influence on the others. They will be tempted in many ways, and for them, going to church and worshiping the Lord will be not joyful.

For those who do not have a foundation of faith, there won't be any growth of their faith or joy in their hearts. These types of people will easily blame others or the church. They are still spiritual infants (1 Corinthians 3:3) or spiritually sick (James 3:15). Because there are many people like this in churches, some churches are not able to act as salt and light in this world.

Everything in the world has a foundation or root, and for our Christian lives, the foundation is very important. But a lot of people do not believe that we must have a firm foundation—a strong root to grow from. This is such a shame and a sin against God. God says, "My people are destroyed from lack of knowledge" (Hosea 4:6) and "A people without understanding will come to ruin" (Hosea 4:14). In Isaiah

5:13, He says, "Therefore my people will go into exile for lack of understanding."

There are three things we must remember about faith and two ways to have this faith. So remember this and have faith. The Bible addresses those who do not truly believe in Jesus Christ, but call Jesus "Lord," in the following way:

> Not everyone who says to me, "**Lord, Lord**," will enter the kingdom of heaven, but only he who does the will of my Father who is in heaven. Many will say to me on that day, "**Lord, Lord**, did we not prophesy in **your** name, and in **your** name drive out demons and perform many miracles?" Then I will tell them plainly, "I never knew you. Away from me, you evildoers!"
> ㅡ Matthew 7:21-23

The Bible says that those who haven't believed in their hearts but have only said, "Lord, Lord," will hear God saying, "I never knew you. Away from me, you evildoers," no matter who they are or what they have done. Even a pastor and even those who have done many miracles in the name of the Lord will not enter the kingdom of God if they haven't believed in their hearts and confessed by their mouths. God's words in Mark 7:21-23 echo what was prophesied in Isaiah 29:13: "These people come near to me with their mouth and honor me with their lips, but their hearts are far from me. Their worship of me is made up only of rules taught by men." So know what faith is about and have faith by believing in your hearts. Confess with your mouth.

> Whoever **acknowledges** me before men, I will also **acknowledge** him before my Father in heaven. But

*whoever **disowns** me before men, I will **disown** him before my Father in heaven.*

누구든지 사람 앞에서 나를 시인하면

Matthew 10:32-33

There are people in church who believe that the knowledge they have is faith. But we have to know who Jesus is and believe Him in our hearts. Even when the disciples of Jesus did not know who Jesus was, the demons clearly knew who He was. That's why the man with the evil spirits shouted, "Jesus, Son of the Most High God," as it is written in Mark 5:7. But even though the evil spirits knew who Jesus was, they did not have salvation. By listening to the Word of God, acknowledging Him, having faith in our hearts, and confessing by mouth, we can have salvation.

The 600 thousand people who followed Moses out of Egypt had heard his message for 40 years. They crossed the Red Sea, drank water from the rock, saw the fire on the Mount Sinai, and heard the voice of God. But only Caleb and Joshua entered the Promised Land. All the others died in the desert because they did not combine what they heard with faith in their hearts:

The message they heard was of no value to them, because those who heard did not combine it with faith.

들은 자가 믿음과 결부시키지 않음

Hebrew 4:2

True faith is understanding the message you have heard or read, believing in your heart, and confessing by mouth what you have come to believe. Confessing by mouth means obedience. The Bible says that even the evil spirit believe that there is one God (James 2:19). But even though the evil spirits know and believe it, they won't be saved. If you truly believe in God, you have to obey the Word of God.

Therefore, true faith is understanding the Word of God intellectually, taking the Word of God into our hearts, and intentionally acting on the Word of God. In other words, faith is about taking Jesus into our hearts and lives as our Lord and Savior and acting upon that faith.

To have salvation by having faith in Jesus, one has to confess by mouth that Jesus is Lord. Confessing that Jesus is Lord is confessing that Jesus came to this earth as a man, that He lived in the town called Nazareth, that is He is the Son of God born to Mary, and that He is your Lord.

There are certain conditions for someone to become <u>lord</u> of someone or something:

1. You have to create it in order to be its <u>lord</u>.
2. You have to pay for it to become its <u>lord</u>.
3. You may become the lord of it by receiving it as a gift.

Jesus created us, paid for us with His blood, and received us as a gift from God; therefore, He is our Lord. This is what we will examine from here on out.

PART 2.
GOSPEL OF SALVATION

*That if you confess with your mouth, "Jesus is
Lord," and believe in your heart that God raised
him from the dead, you will be saved.*
Romans 10:9

CHAPTER 1

JESUS IS OUR LORD

The first step to having faith is confessing that Jesus is your Lord. In Romans 10:9, Paul says that you will be saved if you confess with your mouth, "Jesus is Lord." Our faith has to begin with this confession.

We have to confess that Jesus is the Son of God and our Lord. That is to say, Jesus is the Lord of our lives, the Lord of all that we have, and the Lord of our time.

HE CREATED US AND, THEREFORE, HE IS OUR LORD.

People generally know that the Father God created the universe and mankind. But to be more precise, it is the triune God who created everything. The Bible says that the Father God created all the universe through the Son of God, Jesus.

> *He [God the Father] has spoken to us by his Son ...*
> ***through whom** [Jesus the son] he made the universe.*
> *Hebrews 1:1-2*

The Book of Hebrews tells us that God created the entire universe through Jesus. In other words, the Father God let His Son create the universe. The Son of God created the universe in obedience to God, the Father.

> *For by him all things **were created**: things in heaven*
> *and on earth, visible and invisible, whether thrones or*
> *powers or rulers or authorities; all things **were created***
> *by him and for him.*
> *Colossians 1:16*

Things in heaven and on earth, visible and invisible—all things were created by the Son of God, Jesus. "Invisible" includes things that we cannot see because they too far away, things that are too tiny to see, and all the principles of science (Isaiah 45:18, 48:13). Whether thrones or powers or rulers or authorities, all things were created by Him, says the Bible. This means that even the spiritual entities and the angels were created by the Father God through the Son of God, Jesus. And not only that, but it all was created through and for Him.

We humans were created for Jesus. Everything that has been made and created has its purpose. If it doesn't serve purpose it was created for, it is thrown away. The Bible tells us why Jesus created us like this:

> *Everyone who is called by my name, **whom I created***
> ***for my glory**, whom I **formed** and **made**.*
> *Isaiah 43:7*

🍂 *So whether you eat or drink or whatever you do, do it
    all for **the glory** of God*

                                            1 Corinthians 10:31

God, the Father, created us humans through Jesus for
His glory. The most basic and fundamental requirements for
human life are eating and drinking, but there is something
much more important than those: to live for the glory of
God (Isaiah 42:8, 48:11). There are people in church who
would dishonor God by doing things for their own good or
profits, but God doesn't forgive such behavior, whether in
church (Ecclesiastes 5:1-2; Habakkuk 2:20) or out of church
(1 Samuel 2:30; Acts 12:23).

All creatures, which were created through Jesus, obey
God according to the purposes God has given them. But we
humans do evil and disobey God by not living according to
the purpose for which God created us.

🍂 *Your laws endure to this day, for all things serve you.*
                                            Psalm 119:91

Now then, how about you? Are you living your life for
the purpose God has set?

🍂 *Through him [Jesus] all things **were made**; without
    him [Jesus] nothing was made that has been made.*
                                            John 1:3

The Bible repeatedly says that God created the entire
universe through Jesus. It says that nothing was made
without Jesus. Whether you believe it or not and whether
or not you accept Jesus as your Lord and Savior, the truth is
that even you were created by Jesus. It is Christ Jesus who

gave you this life, who has been taking care of you, and who will take your life at the end.

Whether or not you believe it, Christ Jesus is the One who provides all your needs (Ecclesiastes 5:19). And someday, you will have to stand before Him to be judged (Revelation 20:12). When the time comes, you will have to take full responsibility if you have not glorified Him and did not believe the Lord Jesus who created you and gave you this life (Romans 1:21).

If it is Jesus through whom God created the whole universe, then "the Lord" in Psalm 139: 13 is the Lord Jesus, the Son of God.

The writer of this psalm confesses, "Your throne, O God, will last forever and ever: a scepter of justice will be the scepter of your kingdom." Hebrews 1:8 says that "the Lord" from Psalm 45:6 is Jesus, the Son of God. Also, in Hebrews 1:10, the Bible says that "you" from Psalm 102:25 is the Lord Jesus: "in the beginning you laid the foundations of the earth, and the heavens are the work of your hands." Therefore, Jesus is our Lord.

Based on what's written in Psalm 100: 3, Jesus is our God ("Know that the Lord is God"), our creator ("It is he who made us"), our Lord ("we are his"), our King ("we are his people") and our shepherd ("The sheep of his pasture").

Taking Jesus as our Lord is to confess that Jesus is our God, our creator, our Lord, our King, and our shepherd (Psalm 23:1; John 10:11).

Jesus created us in our mother's womb; therefore, He is our Lord. This has to be confessed first.

> ✄ *Yet for us there is but one God, the Father, from whom all things came and for whom we live; and there is but*

> *one Lord, Jesus Christ, through whom all things came*
> *and through whom we live.*
>
> 1 Corinthians 8:6

All things came from the Father. According to Scripture, all things came from the Father, but also through Jesus Christ. The Bible repeatedly proclaims that all things were created through Jesus Christ. We all came from the Father and through Jesus Christ.

Scientists say that the speed of light is approximately 186,282 miles per second in imperial units. The light can go around the Earth 7.5 times in one second. At this speed, it would take about 3,300 years to get to Earth's closest neighboring planet of the Milky Way and more than 100,000 years to go through the Milky Way. Furthermore, scientists say that there are more than a million portions like Milky Way in the universe.

The Son of God, Jesus, who created the whole universe (which we cannot even imagine) and rules over it, died for me, who is so tiny in comparison to those planets and stars that He created; He died on the cross to pay my debt. He paid the ransom for me, and there way for me to express how much He loves me.

> *I have been crucified with Christ and I no longer live,*
> *but Christ lives in me. The life I live in the body, I live*
> *by faith in the Son of God, who loved me and gave*
> *himself for me*
>
> Galatians 2:20

Scientists have found that there are about 130,000,000 light receptors and 7 million light detecting nerves in the human eye. A human nose can detect and distinguish more than 9,000 odors, and a human tongue can distinguish 1,400 different tastes. All these senses were not made by our parents and could not have been made by them. Jesus created the vast universe and every detail of our bodies. He is the Son of God, our almighty Lord. Amen.

JESUS PAID FOR US; THEREFORE, HE IS OUR LORD.

If you want to be Lord of something, you have to pay for it and make it yours. Jesus paid for us; therefore, He is our Lord.

> ✠ ...*with your blood you* **purchased** *men for God from every tribe and language and people and nation.*
> *Revelation 5:9*

From the time we are born, we become slaves to sin. In Romans 6:17, Paul says that we were once slaves to sin. Adam disobeyed God, committing sin against God, and all his descendants were born in sin.

Not only that, but we were also born into sin and commit sin in our lives, and we have all become slaves to sin. John 8:34 says, "Everyone who sins is a slave to sin." A slave to sin becomes a slave to evil (John 8:44) and a slave to death (Colossians 1:21; Hebrews 2:15; James 4:4). Therefore, if you just live your life as you were born, you will go to hell in the end.

Jesus, being God in His very nature (Philippians 2:6), had pity on us. He knew how we would suffer in hell and came to save us, taking the very nature of a servant and being made in human likeness (Luke 19:10; 1 Timothy 1:15). And by His blood, He paid for us—for our redemption. Whoever acknowledges this truth and believes in Jesus will be set free from slavery to sin and will be blessed to be called "God's child." By believing in Jesus Christ, we glorify the Father who made us to be His children.

> ✘ *You are not your own; you **were bought at a price.** Therefore honor God with your body.*
> *1 Corinthians 6:19-20*

As He died on the cross, He paid for our sins by His blood. He bought us at a price. So if anyone acknowledges this truth and believes in Jesus Christ, then Jesus will become his Lord. According to Isaiah 43:7, we were created for the glory of God. But because of our sins, we fell short of His glory. Jesus paid the price for us; we were bought at the price of His blood. Therefore, whoever believes in Him will glorify the Lord. Jesus paid the price by His blood; therefore, He is our Lord.

WE WERE GIFTED TO JESUS, AND JESUS BECAME OUR LORD.

If you want to own something, you either have to pay a price for it, or it must be gifted to you. At that time, you can become the owner of that thing. The Bible says that the Father has placed everything in Jesus' hands.

> ✘ *The Father loves the Son and has **placed** everything in his hands*
> *John 3:35*

> ✘ *I have revealed you to those whom you **gave** me out of the world. They were yours; you **gave** them to me and they have obeyed your word.*
> *John 17: 6*

God loves His Son and gave Him everything and every man in the world. Through the Word of God, we can know that Jesus is the Lord to whom everything and every man in the world have been given and that He owns us, sustains us, and provides for us.

These are the words of the Bible:

> The Son [Jesus] **is sustaining** all things by his powerful word (Hebrews 1:3)
> In Him [Jesus] all things **hold** together (Colossians 1:17)

Jesus said to His disciples, "All authority in heaven and on earth has been given to me" (Matthew 28:18). Jesus, who has received all authority in heaven and on Earth, is sustaining and providing for all things by His powerful word.

Most scientists say that it is natural that spring comes after winter, summer after spring, night after day, day after night, and so on. But the Bible says that all of these natural phenomena are sustained by Jesus through His powerful word.

There is no pillar that supports this Earth. It is just floating in the air. Here, a few questions arise: how is it possible that the Earth rotates (780Mile/h; 1,248Km/h) and revolves (70,000Mile/h; 112,000Km/h), yet it never moves out of its orbit? How can it float in the air for such a long time? Scientists say that it is possible due to the gravity of the Sun, but the Bible says that even the Sun's gravity is sustained by the powerful word of Jesus.

That man breathes more than 25,000 times a day, that he digests what he eats, that his heart pumps more than 100,000 times a day, that he hears with his ears, that he sees through his eyes are not simply "natural" things; All of this is only possible through Jesus Christ, who sustains everything by his powerful word. The Spirit of God teaches us all these things through the Bible (John 14:26). That is how we come into this knowledge. Jesus is our Lord because He sustains and provides.

> ✎ *I **have upheld** since you were conceived, and **have carried** since your birth.*
>
> Isaiah 46:3

He created us in our mother's wombs, formed us, and gave us birth. The Bible says that He has upheld us since we were conceived and has carried us since our birth. Even though we cannot see or feel how He carries us, the Bible is not wrong or fraudulent. We are not able to see, know, or feel these realities, but the Bible is telling us the truth. Then how should we understand this Bible, and how can we explain it? It is not easy, but I will attempt to explain it through these verses:

In Job 39:13-17, there is a story about the ostrich. An ostrich is a kind of bird but different from other types of birds because it cannot fly. It lays its eggs on the ground, allowing them to stay warm in the sand, and does not mind that its eggs get crushed by other animals. The ostrich does not take care of its young, as if they were not hers and her labor was in vain. How is this possible? Job 39:17 says, "For God did not endow her with wisdom or give her a share of good sense." Because God did not endow the ostrich with wisdom or give her a share of good sense, she does not know how to love or take care of her young.

If God had done the same with us, there would be no one in this world who could survive. But God gave us wisdom and a heart to take care of our children; that is why we love and take care of our children, even when it is painful. And this is what God means by "I upheld" and "I carried."

There may be some who would then, "How can you compare humans with ostriches?" But if you read Daniel 4, you will find records indicating that God gave King Nebuchadnezzar the mind of an animal (Daniel 4:16, 25, 33). Can the Father, who gave King Nebuchadnezzar the mind of an animal, give the mind of an ostrich to our parents? Even though He can, He does not give them the mind of an ostrich, but instead gives them the wisdom to love and take care of us. Therefore, we should always thank God for giving us the blessing to live this life.

> ✍ *Even to your old age and gray hairs I am he, I am he who **will sustain** you. I have made you and I will carry you; I will sustain you and I will rescue you.*
> *Isaiah 46:4*

We can regard this life of ours as not being connected to God, thinking that we can enjoy it if we try hard enough, but this is not true. It is God who sustains us; even through our old age and gray hairs, he sustains and carries us. That He sustains us means that He created us in our mothers' wombs, that He gave us life, and that every breath of ours is made by Him. When the Bible uses such expressions as "sustain" and "carry," it is speaking not only of Christians but of all the people in the world being sustained and carried by God.

The Old Testament refers to God, but the New Testament says that Jesus is the Son of God and that He is God. So those who believe in Jesus Christ give thanks to Jesus in all circumstances (1 Thessalonians 5:18), but those who do not believe in Jesus do not give Him thanks nor give Him the glory; instead, they regard their lives as their own. But the Bible says that those who do not give thanks to the Lord will face judgment (Romans 1:21; Hebrews 9:27).

We cannot see or feel how God carries and sustains us. How, then, are we to explain this? Paul explains it this way in the book of Acts:

> ✝ *For in Him [Jesus] we* **live** *and* **move** *and* **have our being.**
>
> *Acts 17:28*

The Bible says that Christ is the reason we live, move, and exist. Christ is the Son of God; who can deny this? Even though some deny this, the truth remains that we live, move, and exist because of Jesus. Many people haven't yet acknowledged this, but we are all alive because of Jesus Christ.

> ✝ *If it were his intention and he withdrew his spirit and breath, all mankind would perish together and man* **would return to the dust.**
>
> *Job 34:14-15*

The Bible says that if Jesus ceases to sustain all things and stops providing, all creatures will die. The fact we are still alive is evidence that Jesus is still sustaining and providing for all things. We often think that we decide for ourselves when to go or stay, to sit or stand, but this is not true.

In April of 1997, I struggled with dizziness. Every 2 to 3 minutes, I got dizzy, and this happened 8 to 10 times a day. As I got dizzy, I wasn't able to walk, drive, or stand up. Even when I was sitting, I would fall down because of this dizziness. If I got dizzy while I was eating, I couldn't even hold a spoon in my hand. Doctors searched for the cause of my dizziness, but found nothing. I prayed, and after two months, I finally realized something as I read the Bible:

> ✍ *The Son [Jesus]* **is sustaining** *all things by his powerful word.*
>
> *Hebrews 1:3*

> ✍ *I lie down and sleep: I wake again, because the Lord* **sustains me**.
>
> *Psalm 3:5*

> ✍ *In Him [Jesus] all things* **hold** *together.*
>
> *Colossians 1:17*

As I read these verses, I finally realized that this was happening to me because I was not with Him. He is the One who has to hold and carry me. But I was not with Him, which was why I had this illness.

God created all things through His Son, and the Son of God, Jesus Christ, is sustaining all things by His powerful word. When scientists say that the sun is upholding the Earth, this really means that Jesus made the Sun to hold the Earth. The fact that the Earth revolves now exactly as it has always is evidence that Jesus is sustaining all things, even now.

I also realized that I can only sleep, sit, and rise when He carries me (Psalm 139:2). I also realized that I can eat, drive, and walk only when He carries me. There are lots of people, even among Christians, who have not understood that we are in the Lord's hands. Can you stand on your feet now? If your answer is "yes," that means that God is upholding your legs. Even if you didn't notice it, God is the One who gave you sleep yesterday and woke you up today.

God let me suffer with dizziness to let me know that everything was by His grace and not by my own power—just grace from the Lord. The Son of God sustains; He gives us the strength even when we do not notice it. He has given us air to breathe, light to see, and water to drink. We are in His hands, and the Bible says that this is how He carries and holds us.

WE HAVE TO ACCEPT HIM AS OUR LORD.

There might be some of you who would feel too much pressure on this point. But if you don't take Him as your Lord, you will belong to the devil (John 8:44; Galatians 4:8; Ephesians 2:2; 1 John 5:19). There are only two choices for man: to be a servant of God or a servant of the devil (1 John 3:10). Some might say that they do not belong to God or the devil, but themselves. But they only say this because they don't know about the spiritual world. If you haven't taken Jesus as your Lord, then the devil is ruling in your heart as your lord.

Jesus created us. He paid for and purchased us at the price of His blood. We were given to Him from God; therefore, He is our Lord. True faith is gained only when you first admit that Jesus is your Lord. Take Him as your Lord; take Him into your heart and life. Acknowledge that we have sinned in living our lives without Him. Repent of your sins. Take Him into your heart as your Lord. Know that the devil has been in your heart, where Jesus should have lived.

There are sorrows, struggles, evil things, and wars in this world. But not these—not even sicknesses and diseases, nor economical crisis—are the real tragedies of this world. Many people assume that the world will get better with a better leader and that they will have a better life then. But a better leader for this world will just bring some changes, not the essential ones.

A lot of people make such efforts to make a better world, but in that time, the devil gets much more evil, violent, and intellectual. Many scholars talk about human rights, peace, and a benevolent spirit, but these are just words from their mouths. In fact, they are the ones who are selfish, seeking good things for themselves. Why are these kinds of things happening? Isn't there any way to solve this problem?

Only God can solve this problem because He created everything—us humans and the world. The only way to solve this problem is to take Jesus into our hearts as our Savior and Lord. Without Jesus in our hearts as King and Lord, everything will be unhappy. The tragedy of this world is that we all haven't taken Him as our Lord and Savior.

Do you know why this is the only solution? It's because God created us according to His image. God is greater than the universe (Hebrews 3:3), and we were created according to His image (Genesis 1:27). Nothing but the Lord can satisfy us (Proverbs 30:15; Ecclesiastes 2:9-11). The tragedy begins here, as we try to satisfy ourselves with the things of this world. But if we take Jesus, the Son of God who is greater than the universe, into our hearts, then we will be content, and all the problems we have will be solved (Philippians 4:11; 1 Timothy 6:8).

That we take Jesus into our heart means that we let Him come into our hearts as Lord and let Him rule over our deeds, thoughts, and words. If we do not take Him into our hearts as Lord and let him rule over our deeds, thoughts, and words, then our old selves, who have an evil nature to disobey God, will do evil things.

> ✘ *The LORD saw how great man's wickedness on the earth had become, and that every inclination of the thoughts of his heart was only **evil** all the time.*
>
> *Genesis 6:5*

> ✘ *Every inclination of his heart is **evil** from childhood.*
>
> *Genesis 8:21*

> ✘ *The heart is **deceitful** above all things and beyond cure.*
>
> *Jeremiah 17:9*

> ✘ *For from within, out of men's hearts, come **evil thoughts**, sexual immorality, theft, murder, adultery.*
>
> *Mark 7:21*

There are people who believe that man becomes evil, even though man used to be innocent; however, the Bible says that man's heart has been evil <u>from </u>childhood. This is because man was born with a sinful nature—original sin.

Everything exists as they were created by God, except for evil. Evil resists God, and we have disobeyed God. And the Bible says that man's heart is evil and rotten. Because of man's evil heart, plans, and thoughts, it is impossible to have peace in this world without God.

When we talk about the evil heart of man, we usually think about a wicked man or a violent and aggressive man. But the Bible says, "In his thoughts there is no room for God" (Psalm 10:4, 14:1). These verses from the Psalms say that the evil man is the one who has no room for God in his thoughts and life. Therefore, the Bible says that all men who do not believe in Jesus are evil and corrupted (Titus 1:15). Those who do not have in mind the things of God, but the things of man, are evil (Matthew 16:23).

The Bible says, "My people have committed two sins: They have forsaken me, the spring of living water, and have dug their own cisterns, broken cisterns that cannot hold water" (Jeremiah 2:13). Our forsaking of the Lord is a sin. And that we have not leaned on Him is another sin. That we have forsaken Him means that we have not believed in Him or served Him as our Lord. In other words, the Bible is saying that all men who have not taken Jesus into their hearts as Lord are evil (Titus 1:15).

The Bible also says that even those who have taken Jesus as their Lord can do evil things if they do not submit to the Lord and let Him control them. Romans 7:19 says, "For what I do is not the good I want to do: no, the evil I do not want to do - this I keep on doing." If you have taken Jesus into your heart as your Lord, you have to let Him rule over your thoughts and mind. In other words, you have to be filled with the Spirit of God.

God created all things to be under His reign (Isaiah 48:13). But man sinned and refused to be under God's reign. Man tried to live according to his own thoughts and plans. Believing in Jesus Christ basically means that we give glory to God by returning to God, by putting ourselves under His control, as we are made to be.

The reason Jesus came to this earth was to set up the kingdom of God (Daniel 2:44; Mark 1:15; Ephesians 1:10). That is why the most important part from the Lord's Prayer is when it says, "your kingdom come" (Matthew 6:10).

Jesus said that we should seek first His kingdom and His righteousness (Matthew 6:33). Here "his kingdom" means the "kingdom of God", which means that everything has to be under His control and reign.

We know how the Lord's Prayer ends: "For yours is the kingdom and the power and the glory forever" (Matthew 6:13). The "kingdom" is the kingdom of God; in this kingdom, God reigns. The "power" means the power of God. In other words, as we say this part of the Lord's prayer, we pray that we want the kingdom of God to come to us and that we want the power of God to reign. By saying, "and the glory forever," we are saying that the glory will be His as His kingdom comes to us and as He reigns in us; His name will be glorified and His will be done through us.

As you take Jesus into your heart, the kingdom of God will come to you. Then the Lord will reign, and you will be able to glorify the Lord. This is what the Lord's Prayer teaches us, and this is the core of the Lord's Prayer. Do you want to give glory to the Father? Then take Him as your Lord into your heart and let Him reign in your heart and life.

The saints and the saved people will sing "Hallelujah" four times as they enter the wedding banquet with the lamb (Revelation 19:1, 3, 4, 6), but the last one will be "Hallelujah! Salvation and glory and power belong to our God" (Revelation 19:6).

Therefore, taking Jesus as the Lord and Savior is the first, last, and all of our faith. If you don't take Him into your heart as Lord and King, then your life will be just like one from the book of Judges. As the Israelites had peace among them, they left God and started to worship idols. God became angry with them and punished them. Then they repented, and God gave them peace again. But again, they forgot about God, who gave them peace, and started to sin again.

If you repeat the same sin, I tell you that the kingdom of God is not in your heart. If the kingdom of God is not in your heart, this means that you haven't taken Him as your Lord or that you haven't let Him reign in your life.

In the book of Judges, Micah says, "Now I know that the Lord will be good to me" (Judges 17:13), even though he has been serving idols instead of God. He served idols, but believed that God would bless him. There are lots of people like Micah among us. They come to church and call on the name of the Lord, but they do not know what Christianity is all about. They just ask God to give them blessings. Jeremiah 7:2 says that even those who came through those gates to worship the Lord did not know God and did not listen to the Word of God. We are like them. Without knowing who God and Jesus are, it is not possible to have a right relationship with them. Do you want to know who God is? Do you want to believe in Jesus? It's still not too late. You might have been like one of those who did not know God and did not listen to God, but it is not too late yet. The Bible says, "Now is the time of God's favor, now is the day of salvation" (1 Corinthians 6:2).

People from the tribe of the Danites served idols, but they still believed that God would be with them (Judges 18). But through Judges chapters 19 and 20, we see how all of the Israelites had to struggle because of the sin of the Danites. Why did this happen? The Bible says that it happened because they did not have a king; instead, everyone did as he saw fit (Judges 17:6, 18:1, 19:1, 21:25).

The Israelites were looking for a king—a man. But the Bible says that God is king and that He is the Lord (1 Samuel

8:7, 12:12, Psalm 100:3, Isaiah 6:5, Zephaniah 3:15). They rejected God as their king, and the chaos started from that. If man does not have God as king and Lord in his heart, he will do as he sees fit, and there will be only chaos. It does not matter whether he comes to church or not; without Jesus in his heart as the Lord and King, it's meaningless.

The problem in churches also is a result of people not having Jesus as their Lord and King and not allowing Him to reign because they do follow their own will instead (Matthew 16:23; John 16:3; 1 Corinthians 3:3).

Jesus is the light of the world (John 8:12). So not believing Jesus means spiritually staying away from the light. If you stay away from the light, then you are in darkness (John 9:4, 11:10; Ephesians 5:8). In the darkness, you cannot see clearly to find a way and, therefore, might go the wrong way easily. Without Jesus as our king and Lord, we will live in fear and anxiety. Colossians 2:6 says, "So then, just as you received Christ Jesus as Lord, continue to live in him." This means that you have to put yourself under his control.

If you want Jesus to reign in your life, you have to crucify your old self and sinful nature with Christ and let Christ live in you (Galatians 2:20, 5:24). Then Jesus will become your king.

It is not something we can do from the very first time we start to believe in Jesus. After we take Him as our Lord and King, we have to offer ourselves to Him (Romans 6:13) and pray; God will then bring changes into our lives. The Bible says, "Have nothing to do with godless myths and old wives' tales: rather, train yourself to be godly" (1 Timothy 4:7). Meditate on the Word of God and pray every day. Train yourself and experience how the Spirit of God changes you

(2 Corinthians 3:18). As you train yourself, you will have holy habits, and these holy habits will change you.

The Bible says that man can reject God as his King and Lord while he's still living in this world, but that after death, every knee will bow and every tongue confess that Jesus Christ is Lord. All those in heaven and on earth and under the earth will do so.

> ✠ *That at the name of Jesus every knee should bow, in heaven and on earth and under the earth, and every tongue confess that Jesus Christ is Lord, to **the glory** of God the Father.*
>
> *Philippians 2:10-11*

After we die, we all have to kneel down before the Lord, whether we believed in Jesus or not, and confess that Jesus Christ is Lord. (Psalm 22:29). Jesus created us, so we cannot make any changes to His plan. God, who destined us to die once, has destined that every knee will bow and every tongue will confess that Jesus Christ is Lord. All men are destined to die once (Hebrews 9:27); this is true. And it is also true that all men will have to kneel down and confess that Jesus Christ is Lord.

Those who believe in Jesus Christ while on this earth will confess that Jesus Christ is Lord before the judgment seat and then enter into heaven. Those who have rejected Him will also have to confess that Jesus Christ is Lord, but they will enter into hell and suffer in pain forever.

> **Do you want to confess that Jesus Christ is Lord now, while in this world, and enter into heaven? Or do you still want to reject Jesus and enter hell after the Judgment?**

The Life of those who have confessed that Jesus Christ is Lord

If one, who used to follow the ways of this world and of the ruler of the kingdom of the air—the devil(Ephesians 2:2; 1 John 5:19)— confesses that Jesus Christ is his Lord, then his life should be changed. In other words, if you have taken Jesus Christ as your Lord, you have let Him be your King and Lord.

> ✘ You are **my servant**, O Israel. I have made you, you are **my servant**.
>
> Isaiah 44:21

> ✘ Your laws endure to this day for all things serve you.
> Psalm 119:91

All creatures have become servants of Jesus. This is the first thing we have to admit, believe, and confess. But Adam, wanting to be like God, ate the fruit from the tree of good and evil and, as a result, sin was passed on to all of his descendants. Ever since Adam committed this sin, we have forgotten that we are creatures of God and have lived our lives as we saw fit. But servants should not live like that. Servants should follow the will of their master.

> ✘ Why do you call me, 'Lord, Lord," and **do not do** what I say?
>
> Luke 6:46

A lot of people who followed Jesus called Him, "Lord, Lord," but they did not do what Jesus said. If you have confessed that Jesus Christ is Lord, then you have to obey what He says. He is the Son of God, but still He said, "By myself I can do nothing" (John 5:30). Even in the matter of His death, He prayed to God: "Everything is possible for you. Take this cup from me. Yet not what I will, but what you will." (Mark 14:36). He himself became a model for us and showed us how to obey God. If you do not do what He says, your confession that Jesus Christ is Lord is meaningless.

If you have confessed that Jesus Christ is your Lord, King, and Shepherd, then the One who sustains all things by His powerful words will guide you, protect you, walk with you, and be with you forever. Then your life will be peaceful, safe, and fruitful. That is why and how King David confessed Psalm 23:4, "Even though I walk through the valley of the shadow of death, I will fear no evil." Jesus will take care of you, and you will not have to fear anything. Those who have taken Jesus as their Lord and King should know that Jesus is spiritual and physical blessing for us. Psalm 16:2 says, "You are my Lord: apart from you I have no good thing." King David confessed that God was his Lord and that he could not have anything good apart from Him.

This is why we have to obey the Word of God. These principles can be summarized as follows:

+ Jesus Christ is the one who gave me this life.
+ Jesus has bought me with His blood.
+ Jesus is the one who sustains all things by His powerful words.

Many times, we think that we are living for ourselves. But we are living for Christ. Because He is the one who created us, He rules, and He is the one who will take my life, after all. Soon, we will stand before the seat of judgment and confess that Jesus Christ is Lord (Romans 14:11; Philippians

2:10-11), and we will enter heaven to live with God forever. We are His, and our lives are in His hands. This is what we have to admit, believe, and lean on. We have to learn from Jesus, the One who prayed and sought the will of God.

> ⚰ *For none of us lives to himself alone and none of us dies to himself alone. If we live, we live to the Lord; and if we die, we die to the Lord. So, whether we live or die, we belong to the Lord.*
>
> *Romans 14:7-8*

> ⚰ *Christ will be exalted in my body, whether by life or by death. For to me, to live is Christ and to die is gain.*
> *Philippians 1:20-21*

The apostle Paul, who knew of divine providence well, knew also that living and dying are in the hands of Christ (Deuteronomy 33:3; Jeremiah 18:6). Paul says that all things were created by Him and for Him (Colossians 1:16) and for His glory (Isaiah 43:7). Paul also says that God purposed in Christ to bring all things in heaven and on earth together under one head, even Christ (Ephesians 1:10). As all things on earth and in heaven allow Jesus to reign as King and Lord, the will and plan of God to bring all things together under one head will be accomplished.

In Revelation 11:15, we see that the seventh angel will sound his trumpet, and there will be loud voices in heaven, which say, "The kingdom of the world has become the kingdom of our Lord and of his Christ, and he will reign forever and ever." God and Jesus planned to be king and Lord forever and ever. Therefore, we should serve God and Jesus as King and Lord. If you don't believe in this and accept the plan of God, there will be only the wrath of God for you.

Give your heart to the Lord and let Him reign. Give Him the glory and let Him be glorified through you: this is what we should do throughout all of our lives.

> ✍ Praise the Lord, **all his works** everywhere in his **dominion**. Praise the Lord, o my soul.
>
> *Psalm 103:22*

All things and all men were created by Jesus, and they are still living in the place where Jesus reigns. Therefore, all men should believe in Him, fear Him, love Him, and praise Him.

We people tend to think that we are the most important ones in this world. We say that the world and others exist for me. We regard everything meaningless without us. We have put ourselves in the center because we are selfish. But the world would still be here, even without us. The stars, the moon, and the sun would still be there even without us. But without Jesus Christ, the world, the stars, the moon, and the sun cannot exist. Jesus is the precious and worthy One. We each have to take Him into the center of our heart and love Him (Matthew 22:37). We have to give Him the honor and glory, which is how we confess that Jesus Christ is Lord (Revelation 5:13)

Paul prayed this for the saints in Ephesus: "…that Christ may dwell in your hearts through faith. And I pray that you, being rooted and established in love…" (Ephesians 3:17). The saints in Ephesus were chosen (Ephesians 1:4). They had forgiveness of sins (Ephesians 1:7) and were marked in Him with a seal (Ephesians 1:13). They had been saved by grace (Ephesians 2:8), and they were fellow citizens with God's people and members of God's household (Ephesians 2:19). Christ lived in them (1 John 3:24), and this is how they were. So why did Paul pray for them to have Christ in their hearts?

He prayed this because of those people who hadn't taken Jesus into the center of their hearts and who wouldn't let Jesus reign in their lives. With bitterness, rage, anger, brawling, and slander, along with every form of malice, they committed sins. They were not kind, compassionate, or forgiving to one another, as Christ had been towards them (Ephesians 4:30-32).

What about you? Have you allowed Jesus to reign in your life?

There are people who make Jesus wait at the door. Even though they confess that Jesus Christ is Lord, they themselves have become the Lord of their lives. But God says that He is about to spit those kind of people out of His mouth because they are lukewarm—j neither hot nor cold (Revelation 3:16).

Those kind of people say, "I am rich: I have acquired wealth and do not need a thing" (Revelation 3:17). Many people came to this church, and everything seemed to be going well. To us, this church would seem to be one of the best churches, worthy of praise. But God says, "But you do not realize that you are wretched, pitiful, poor, blind and naked....So be earnest, and repent" (Revelation 3:17-19). The people of this church took themselves to be good Christians, but they were not in the eyes of God.

There are still churches like this and people like them. Why are they lukewarm? The Bible gives us this reason:

> ✘ Here I am! I stand at the door and knock. If anyone
> hears my voice and **opens the door**, I will come in and
> eat with him, and he with me.
>
> *Revelation 3:20*

Jesus is knocking on your heart. There are people who make Jesus wait at the door for five years, ten years, and even longer. When a friend of theirs comes to them, they will not hesitate to open the door. But when Jesus, the Son of God—the One who has paid for them and bought them with His blood, the One who wants to give them His grace and love—comes to the door, they won't open but instead, make him wait. Have you still not opened the door to Him? If not, there is no doubt that you do not have salvation yet.

> ✍ Yet to **all who received him**, to those who believed in
> his name, he gave the right to become children of God.
> *John 1:12*

The Bible says that faith is receiving Jesus <u>in</u> your heart. Even though I was a Christian, I made Jesus wait for me for 30 years. I let Him stand at the door and wait for me. I was born in a Christian family. And although I was a Christian, I did not have Jesus in my heart. I hope that there will no longer be people like I was.

> ✍ If anyone acknowledges that Jesus is **the Son of God**,
> God lives in him and he in God.
> *1 John 4:15*

Therefore, we have to take Him into our hearts as our Lord. To be able to do so, we first have to confess that Jesus is the Son of God and our Lord.

We can see that what Paul wrote in Romans 10:10 correlates to what John wrote in 1 John 4:15. Both verses tell us that we have to take Jesus as Lord and let Him reign.

Jesus has to be our priority, and He has to be glorified through us.

Have you taken Jesus into your heart?
Or have you been making Him wait at the door?

CHAPTER 2

THE DEATH OF CHRIST ON THE CROSS AS REDEMPTION

The second part of believing in Jesus Christ is believing in the death of Christ on the cross as redemption. This means that Jesus took all our sins and died for us, in our place. He paid for us by His death.

Why did sinless Jesus die in our place? Why did He pay for us to gain our redemption? There is a deep relationship between Jesus and us: He is the One who created us according to His image. He is the One who gives us life, breath, and everything else (Acts 17:25).

But because of our sinful nature, we have ignored this truth and regarded ourselves apart from Him. Our parents didn't give us life. Our parents didn't pay our debt on the cross. Only Jesus has opened a way for us by dying on the cross for us, paying our debts, and taking away all of our sins. Jesus loves us more than anybody else.

Then how has He revealed His love and righteousness to the world? He has revealed His great love and righteousness to us by His death on the cross.

We are all sinners before God. There is no one who is not a sinner. One might say that he has lived without sin, but he is only able to say this because he does not know the nature of sin or who he is. All people are born into original sin which is incorporated into Adam. The problems of original sin (Romans 5:12) and sins that we have committed (Titus 3:3) have to be solved in order for us to enter into heaven.

> *For all **have sinned** and fall short of the glory of God.*
> *Romans 3:23*

God says that all men living in this world have sinned. The form of the sin might be different, but all men are sinners. Anyone who claims that he is not a sinner is only able to say so because he hasn't met the Holy God (Isaiah 6:5) or because he does not know of spiritual things (Luke5:8). They are deceived by the devil (John 8:44; 2 Corinthians 4:4; Ephesians 4:18-19; 1John 5:19) and claim that they have not sinned. Like Pharisees, they think that they are righteous and claim that they are sinless (Luke 18:11).

But the Bible says that we deceive ourselves and that the truth is not in us if we claim to be without sin (1 John 1:8); it also says that we make God out to be a liar (1 John 1:10). If we claim that we have not sinned, His Word has no place in our lives.

> *For the wages of sin is **death**.*
> *Romans 6:23*

No matter what kind of sin, there is a wage for all sin. And it does not matter how often and how much you have sinned; the wages of sin is death. Without Jesus Christ, all men who have sinned will go to hell. There is no one righteous before God, not even one (Romans 3:10; Isaiah 64:6; Ecclesiastes 7:20).

We regard sin as something that appears in our behavior. But the Bible says that even having wrongful thoughts is a sin.

> ✘ *You have heard that it was said to the people long ago, 'Do not murder, and anyone who murders will be subject to judgment.' But I tell you that* **anyone who is angry** *with his brother will be subject to judgment. Again,* **anyone who says to his brother, 'Raca,'** *is answerable to the Sanhedrin. But* **anyone who says, 'You fool!'** *will be in danger of the fire of hell.*
> *Matthew 5:21-22*

The sixth commandment that God gave to the Israelites is, "Do not murder." The Israelites regarded murder as killing others with weapons or by their hands. But Jesus said that even getting angry with a brother would be subject to judgment. Jesus said that saying "*Raca*" or "you fool" is the same as murdering.

> ✘ **Anyone who hates** *his brother is* **a murderer,** *and you know that no murderer has eternal life in him.*
> *1 John 3:15*

Jesus says that hating someone is murder and that no murderer has eternal life in him; this means that the one who hates his brother is not saved. Even though you have not killed someone with a knife, you are a murderer if you have hated someone. And if you have hated someone, there is no eternal life in you. There are wives who hate their husbands. But you have to know that by hating your husband, you have killed him—you have become a murderer. It is the same with husbands who hate their wives; they have killed their wives. Jesus also mentioned about the seventh commandment.

> ✘ *But I tell you that anyone who looks at a woman lustfully has already **committed adultery** with her in his heart.*
>
> *Matthew 5:28*

To Jews, committing adultery was having sex with someone other than their spouse. But Jesus said that just looking at a woman lustfully is adultery. So, even when you have not passed from thoughts to action, just having wrongful thoughts is a sin before God.

You have sinned by your thoughts up until now. Adding to that, you have original sin and other sins you have committed. There is no one who can say, "I am righteous" before God. There is no one righteous before God, not even one (Romans 3:10; Ecclesiastes 7:20).

> ✘ *Anyone, then, who knows the good he ought to do and doesn't do it, **sins**.*
>
> *James 4:17*

Everyone knows that it is a sin when a man does an evil thing. But the Bible says that not doing good is also a sin (Matthew 25:40). We say that one has grown up spiritually when we see that he no longer hates someone he used to hate. But as a Christian, we should not stop at that. We should love that someone we used to hate. He who has been stealing must steal no longer, but must work—doing something useful with his own hands—that he may have something to share with those in need.(Ephesians 4:28)

It's a sin if you do not love even when you know you should love one another. Love is the greatest commandment, so not loving one another is a great sin (Romans 13:8, James 2:8).

> ✍ *In regard to sin, because men **do not believe in me**.*
> *John 16:9*

Many people think that believing in Jesus is a choice. They regard Christianity as a religion they have chosen to follow. They think they chose to believe in Jesus. However, it is not a choice, but something that all men have to do. We were created to live in fellowship with God. If we have a broken relationship with God, we will die spiritually. All men have sinned (Romans 5:12), and we are dead in our transgressions and sins (Ephesians 2:1). Jesus came to restore our relationship to God and to give us spiritual life.

So whoever wants to live spiritually has to believe in Jesus (John 3:3, 16). There is no better good news than this. Taking this good news and believing in Jesus Christ is the best thing, but rejecting it is a sin. If you believe in Jesus Christ, your sin will be forgiven. But if you don't, your sins will not be forgiven. So based on what's written in John 16:9, we can say this:

> *Man goes to hell not because of his sins, but because*
> *he does not believe in Jesus Christ.*

Not doing what God has told us to do is a sin, and doing what God has told us not to do is also a sin. God has told us to believe in Jesus; therefore, not believing in Jesus is disobeying God—a sin.

> *Judah's sin is engraved with an iron tool, inscribed with a flint point, on* **the tablets of their hearts** *and on* **the horns of their altars.**

Jeremiah 17:1

The Bible says that sin is engraved and inscribed on the tablets of the people's hearts and on the horns of their altars. Many people regard these words as merely a symbol. They do not think that this would really happen. But the Bible says that Judah's sin is engraved and inscribed on the tablets of their hearts and on the horns of their altars.

Chapters 1 to 5 of Leviticus show us the five typical offerings, and in chapter 4, we read about the sin offering. For the other four offerings, the people are not told to put blood on the horns of the altar. But for the sin offering, God said, "… put some of the blood on the horns of the altar …" (Leviticus 4:7, 18, 25, 30, 34, 16:18). The sin offering is an offering for the sins of the people. "Without the shedding of blood there is no forgiveness," says Hebrews 9:22. The priest put blood on the horns of the altar in order to have the people's sins washed away.

From the ~~Leviticus 29:10~~ Exodus 12 to Ezekiel 43:20, every time a sin offering was brought, some of blood had to be put on the horns of the altar, and the reason God commanded this was because God engraved the sin on the horns of the altar (Jeremiah 17:1, Revelation 9:13). Later, we will talk about the sin engraved on the tablets of our hearts. But the Bible says that the sin engraved on the horns of the altar and on the tablets of our hearts cannot be removed by anything else.

> ✎ *"Although you wash yourself with **soda** and use an abundance of **soap**, the stain of your **guilt** is still before me," declares the Sovereign Lord.*
>
> Jeremiah 2:22

The Bible says that sin cannot be washed even with soda and soap: this means that the problem of sin cannot be solved by any of self-discipline, good deeds, efforts, or self-mortification. There are some who say that people will be saved by their good deeds, even though they regard the Bible as the Word of God (Romans 3:12; Galatians 2:16). They say that they know God, but they are in error because they do not know God and the Bible—the Word of God. They are just revealing their thoughts (Matthew 22:29; John 7:28).

Namely, there is no way to get rid of the sin that has been engraved on the tablets of our hearts and on the horns of the altar. And without having the problem of sin solved, no one can enter the kingdom of God. But we have to know this: that God can do what man cannot do. "What is impossible with men is possible with God" (Luke 18:27). God taught us how we can have our sins washed away.

> ✎ *For the life of a creature is in **the blood**, and I have given it to you to make atonement for yourselves on the altar: it is **the blood** that makes atonement for one's life*
>
> Leviticus 17:11

Our sin cannot be washed with soda or with soap. But God has taught us that sin can be washed by blood, for the life of a creature is in the blood. Without the shedding of blood, there is no forgiveness (Hebrews 9:22).

58

Blood = Life // Sin = Death

If a man who will die because of sin wants to live, he can have a new life by the blood. All men have sinned, and they go to their deaths. All men have sinned, and they have blood that goes to death. In order for a man who has sinned to gain new life, he must have sinless blood. To solve the problem of sin, we need the blood of someone who is spotless and sinless. But there is no one who has spotless and sinless blood (Romans 3:23, 5:12).

If this is true, then how can this sin problem be solved? If there is no one who has spotless and sinless blood, should we bring the blood of an animal to the altar as an atonement offering? The Bible says that it is impossible for the blood of animals to take away sins.

> ✘ *Because it is impossible for the blood of bulls and goats to take away* ***sins***.
>
> *Hebrews 10:4*

> ✘ *Day after day every priest stands and performs his religious duties; again and again he offers the same sacrifices [all in the Old Testament], which can never take away* ***sins***.
>
> *Hebrews 10:11*

In Leviticus 16, God says that in order to have sins washed and forgiven, a bull has to be offered for the priest and goats for the people. The Old Testament says that by the offering of the blood of an animal, sins will be washed (Leviticus 16:30). Leviticus 4 also says that sin will be forgiven through the blood of a sin offering (Leviticus 4:20, 26, and 31). But the writer of Hebrews says that it is impossible for the blood of bulls and goats to take away sins. Is the Old Testament saying something different from the New Testament?

The word *atonement* (*kaphar*) in the Old Testament means "to cover." In other words, God covers the sins of the people as they bring atonement offerings with blood because He, in his forbearance, had left the sins committed beforehand unpunished (Romans 3:25, Hebrews 9:15). The sins that had been covered by God in His forbearance are forgiven by the blood of Jesus Christ. But the sins that were not covered in the time of the Old Testament will not be forgiven, not even by the blood of Jesus Christ. The sins God has covered are washed by the blood of Jesus Christ, and that is why God declared that they would be forgiven in the time of the Old Testament.

So the Old Testament and New Testament are not saying something different; rather, the New Testament is explaining this truth more accurately in Hebrews. The Son of God was conceived by the Virgin Mary through the Spirit of God, and He is spotless and sinless; so is His blood.

> ✄ *But with the precious blood of Christ, a lamb **without blemish or defect**.*
>
> 1 Peter 1:19

That Jesus is a lamb without blemish or defect means that He was born by the Spirit of God through the Virgin Mary and that He is, therefore, sinless. Yes, this is true. But we still question this truth. Mary was a sinner just like us, even though the Catholic Church says that she was sinless. Because Jesus was born through her, we think that He took blood from her. But if He were born with the blood of a sinner—Mary—He would not have been able to save us.

If Jesus were born with sins, then the redemption of the Christians would not have been possible.

So how can this problem be solved? If Mary was a sinner just like us, how is it possible that Jesus was born without sins? Like many, I spent much time trying to answer this question. But modern scientists have verified that not even a drop of a pregnant mother's blood is transferred to the fetus in the womb; this fact gave me the answer to my questions. You can find out more about this in a book called *The Chemistry of the Blood*, written by M. R. De Haan, M.D.

> During the normal course of a pregnancy, the mother's and baby's blood does not mix or circulate together. And the blood of the fetus is from the fetus itself, not from the mother.[1]

I contacted three doctors after I read this book and asked them about this. All three doctors confirmed that the blood of a mother and the blood of the fetus do not mix or circulate. The fetus gets nutrition through the umbilical cord. Oxygen and nutrients in the maternal blood diffuse through the walls of the villi and enter the fetal capillaries, but the mother's and baby's blood do not mix or circulate together. The Bible says that there is life in blood. So even when Mary was a sinner, Jesus was not born with sin because He did not have blood from her. He is sinless; He does not have original sin like we do.

That Jesus is a lamb without blemish and defect also means that He did not sin at all while He was living in this world. He was tempted in many ways. After 40 days of fasting,

---

1   M. R. De Haan, *The Chemistry of the Blood* (Grand Rapids: The Zondervan Publishing House, 1943), 30-31.

He was tested by the devil, but He won. He withstood the test by the woman who got caught committing adultery. Two days before He died, He withstood the test of the question about taxes by saying, "Give to Caesar what is Caesar's and to God what is God's." He was tempted and tested, but He withstood all of that and won. He is spotless and sinless.

> ✘ ...*One who has been tempted in every way, just as we are -- yet was **without sin.***
>
> *Hebrews 4:15*

The Bible says that He was tempted in every way like us, yet was without sin: He is spotless and sinless.

> ✘ *But you know that he appeared so that he might take away our **sins**. And in him is no **sin**.*
>
> *1 John 3:5*

These words of God say that Jesus does not have original sin, nor has he committed any sin. Only the blood of Jesus Christ, who is spotless and sinless, can wash our sins. The blood of Christ shed on the cross solves the problem of our sins. The founders of other religions cannot wash our sins because they are creatures of God, just like us. They cannot die for us and pay for our redemption in order to save us. As you believe that only the blood of Jesus Christ can wash your sin and save you, the Spirit of God will wash the sin that has been engraved on the tablets of your hearts.

> ✘ *How much more, then, will **the blood** of Christ, who through the eternal **Spirit** offered himself unblemished to God, cleanse our consciences from acts that lead to death, so that we may serve the living God.*
>
> *Hebrews 9:14*

🖎 ...who have been chosen according to the foreknowledge of God the Father, through the sanctifying work of the Spirit, for obedience to Jesus Christ and **sprinkling by his blood**: Grace and peace be yours in abundance.

1 Peter 1:2

🖎 Let us draw near to God with a sincere heart in full assurance of faith, **having our hearts sprinkled** to cleanse us from a guilty conscience and having our bodies washed with pure water

Hebrews 10:22

Those who believe in Jesus Christ will have redemption through his blood—the forgiveness of sins—in accordance with the riches of God's grace (Ephesians 1:7, Colossians 1:14).

The Bible says that our sins are engraved on the tablets of our hearts (Jeremiah 17:1), but the Spirit of God will sprinkle the blood of Christ on those who have faith in order to cleanse their sins. The Bible says that it will be sprinkled on the hearts of men and on their heads because sin is engraved on the heart of man. Even though we cannot see this with our own eyes, feel it, or prove it with any evidence theologically, we have to believe in this truth because we heard it through the Word of God.

Not only that, but the Bible also says that Jesus paid the price for us with His blood (Hebrews 9:14 - He offered himself unblemished to God, not to the devil). No matter what kind of sin, all sin has its wages.

🖎 ...With **your blood you purchased** men for God from every tribe and language and people and nation.

Revelation 5:9

Because of our sins, we should be put to death. But for us to be able to enter the kingdom of God, He sent His only Son, who died on the cross and paid for us with His blood. Therefore, you have to confess this with your mouth: Jesus paid for your sins and you are His. Believe in this truth, and you will be saved. This is possible because God so loves us (Ephesians 5:2; Romans 5:8; 1 John 4:10).

The Bible says that the blood of Jesus Christ will cleanse the sins of all people who believe in Him—the blood that He shed on the cross. If it were just the blood of Christ that we needed to have our sins washed, then Jesus did not have to be crucified; people could have just cut him and let Him bleed. But the Bible says that only the blood of Christ from the cross can cleanse sins and save people.

Why? Because He took all of our transgressions, iniquities, and curses as He was pierced on the cross. If man commits sin, God curses him (Deuteronomy 27:26; Galatians 3:10). Sin is that horrible. We are cursed because Adam sinned (Genesis 3:19), and because we have sinned, we are cursed (Deuteronomy 27:26, Galatians 3:13). By His death on the cross, Jesus has not only taken our sins away, but has also removed the curse that was upon us.

> …*Anyone who is hung on a tree is under God's* **curse**.
> *Deuteronomy 21:23*

This word that God gave us through Moses says that anyone who is hung on a tree is under God's curse. Jesus was killed by hanging on a tree (Acts 5:30, 13:29; 1 Peter 2:24). Romans killed Him by hanging on a tree according to their laws, but this was all prophesied through Moses 1,400 years before Christ's death.

> ✘ *Christ redeemed us from **the curse** of the law by becoming **a curse** for us, for it is written: "**Cursed** is everyone who is hung on a tree."*
>
> *Galatians 3:13*

The apostle Paul says that the prophecy in Deuteronomy 21:23 was fulfilled through the death of Christ on the cross. We were actually sinners who were about to be put to eternal death and were by nature objects of wrath (Ephesians 2:3). But through faith in Jesus Christ, we were set free from the curse and are now new creatures—the children of God.

Therefore, there is now no condemnation for those who are in Christ Jesus (Romans 8:1). We now have received God's abundant provision of grace and the gift of righteousness (Romans 5:10); the Bible says this because Jesus has settled the curse and our sins.

> ✘ *Therefore, if anyone is in Christ, he is **a new creation**: the old has gone, **the new** has come!*
>
> *2 Corinthians 5:17*

We became a new creation as we put our faith in Jesus Christ. We have a different quality now. Believing in Jesus Christ will not only solve the problem of sin, but also the curse and condemnation; all of these difficult spiritual problems will be solved. Our body is the same as before, but through faith in Jesus Christ, we have a different spiritual quality: we have become a new creation.

Those who believe in Jesus Christ do not need to look for a fortuneteller because one is not needed. Some people say that they have to get rid of the curse in the family (Exodus 20:5; 1 King 23:26). Because of what is written in the Bible, this sounds right. But to understand the Bible, we have to read the whole Bible. God truly does not want us to stay cursed (Deuteronomy 24:16; 2 King 14:6; Jeremiah 31:30; Ezekiel 18:20).

The Bible says that God saw Adam and all that He had made, and it was very good (Genesis 1:31). But after Adam sinned, God said to Adam, "You are dust." The sin we commit and our sinful minds are hostile towards God (Romans 8:7; Colossians 1:21). This makes our relationship to God a broken one and makes us enemies of God. The Bible says that this broken relationship with God is the death of our spirit (Matthew 8:22; Luke 9:60; Ephesians 2:1). With our spirit dead, only the body made out of dust remains. That is why God told Adam that he was dust. This is the curse of original sin. But Jesus took our curse away, and we are set free by Him.

The Bible says that the life of Jesus is revealed in our body (2 Corinthians 4:10), and the life of Jesus is eternal (1 John 2:25). Those who have the life of Jesus Christ are the children of God (Matthew 16:26, John1:12, 1 John 3:1). Those who do not believe in Jesus Christ are only dust to God. In other words, it does not matter what authority man has, how well educated he is, or how respected and honored he is; if man does not believe in Jesus Christ, man is nothing but dust to God. Even when a man has wealth, he is just dust without Jesus in his heart. But even when a man is poor, not well educated, and has no power or authority, if he believes in Jesus Christ, he is called a child of God (1 John 3:1). Hallelujah!

There will be a huge spiritual change in a man's life if he puts his faith in Jesus Christ. But unfortunately, there are lots of people among Christians who have not come into this knowledge; they just go to church without knowing this truth. Are you saved by your faith in Jesus Christ? If so, do not worry about what others say because you are His precious child (1 John 3:1). Jesus died on the cross for you to make you a child of God.

Are you just dust to God?

Or are you a child of God?

CHAPTER 3
THE RESURRECTION OF THE BODY OF CHRIST

The third thing we are going to talk about is the resurrection of the body of Christ. The resurrection of the body of Christ is the historical truth. We have not seen this with our eyes, and we may not be able to understand it with our knowledge and wisdom. But it is the truth, and we have to believe it. We couldn't see Abraham Lincoln, but because of the historical truth, we believe that he was President of the United States. We did not see the resurrection of the body of Christ, but it has been passed on to us by people who saw; it is the historical truth, and we should believe this.

There are people among Christians who believe in the resurrection of the spirit but not in the resurrection of the body of Christ. But if you do not believe that Jesus came in the flesh (1 John 4:2) and that He rose again from the dead (Luke 24:39), you are not saved (1 John 4:3). The resurrection of the body of Christ is important, and that is why the disciples witnessed it (Acts 26:8).

✘ *And if Christ has not been **raised**, our faith is futile:*
   you are still in your sins.

1 Corinthians 15:17

We generally say that sin has been washed by the death of Christ on the cross. The Bible also says this (Colossians 2:15), and most preachers preach it. But 1 Corinthians 15:17 says that our faith is futile and we are still in our sins if there was no resurrection of Christ. What does this mean? Has Jesus not washed our sins on the cross?

To understand this more easily, you have to combine what is written in Leviticus chapter 16. I will explain more about this passage later on. If you try to understand in combination with Leviticus, you will find that the death of Christ is just a part of His ministry for salvation, but not the whole. The Spirit of God says through Paul in 1 Corinthians 15:17, "And if Christ has not been raised, your faith is futile: you are still in your sins."

But in spite of all this, we still have to know that the death of Christ is the main part of Jesus' ministry that shows us the righteousness and love of God. The most important part of the salvation and the one and only way to have our sins washed is the blood of Christ. The cross is the place where Jesus shed all His blood, and it is, therefore, considered to be the core of salvation. That is why we declare that the problem of sins has been solved by the cross.

In order to have our sins washed and to have salvation, we have to believe in Jesus—what He has done and who He is. Of course, we can say that it's done and given with just one thing. For example, we have to believe in Jesus Christ to receive salvation, but we sometimes say that the one who believes in Jesus is saved. All plans, the process, and the completion of the salvation are in the hands of God. So if one is done among many, the others will be done by God. That is why we sometimes say that one is saved by believing in the cross.

> ⚱ *He was delivered over to death for our sins and was raised to life for our **justification**.*
>
> *Romans 4:25*

Even this word from Romans 4:25 says that without Jesus' resurrection, we would not be justified. To be justified means that our sins are washed, that our relationship with God has been restored, and that we have peace with God so that we can have fellowship with Him.

God raised Jesus from the dead in order to justify us. Without justification, we cannot enter into heaven. In other words, we cannot enter the kingdom of God without the resurrection of Jesus Christ. We may think that the problem of sins was solved on the cross so that we become justified by having faith in the death of the Christ on the cross. But without the resurrection of the Christ, this is meaningless. The resurrection of Jesus Christ has solved the problem of sins and has justified us. The problem of sins has to be solved so that we may enter the kingdom of God and be justified. So the resurrection of Jesus is very closely related to our salvation and is very important.

> ⚱ *In regard to **righteousness**, because I am **going** to the Father, where you can see me no longer.*
>
> *John 16:10*

This is what Jesus told His disciples on the night before He was betrayed. He also told them that He would send them the Counselor, the Spirit of God, and that when He came, He would convict the world in regards to sin, righteousness, and judgment. In saying that the Counselor would convict the world in regards to righteousness, Jesus meant that His disciples would not be able to see Him again because He was going to the Father.

Some biblical scholars believe that the Jews crucified Jesus because they regarded Him as unrighteous. But God raised Him from the dead because He considered Jesus to be righteous, took Jesus to the Father, and seated Him on the right side of God. This interpretation is right.

But there is much more than that in these Words. We actually have to interpret Jesus as saying, "You won't be able to see me again because I am going to the Father to justify you."

So what is the correlation between Jesus going to the Father and people being justified? I will explore this idea now.

> ✻ *Therefore, since we have a great high priest who has*
> ***gone through the heavens***, *Jesus the Son of God, let*
> *us hold firmly to the faith we profess.*
>
> *Hebrews 4:14*

Chapters 1 to 7 of Hebrews explain why Jesus deserves to be our high priest. The Old Testament says that even if one is a descendant of Aaron, if he has any defect, then he cannot be a priest: "No descendant of Aaron the priest who has any defect is to come near to present the offerings made to the LORD by fire. He has a defect; he must not come near to offer the food of his God" (~~Jeremiah~~ *Leviticus* 21:21). Jesus is the One without any defect. The writer of Hebrews says that the high priest who will represent our sin to God is the One who has gone through the heavens—Jesus, the Son of

71

God. This echoes what is written in John 16:10: "I am going to the Father."

The Bible says that we must confess and profess that Jesus went to the Father and became the high priest for us; we are saved by our faith. And to the confession of this faith must be included the acknowledgement that Jesus went to the Father and became the high priest for us. There are people who would see the importance in professing and confessing that Jesus is our high priest, but the Bible says that it has to be a part of our confession. Not only that, but the Bible also says that we have to stand firm in this truth: Jesus is the Son of God, has gone through heaven to the Father, and is now the high priest for us.

> ✘ *If he were on earth, he would not be a priest*
> *Hebrews 8:4*

The Bible says that if He were on earth, He would not be a priest. Jesus went through the heavens to the Father to become our high priest, just as He said in John 16:10, "I am going to the Father." We cannot understand this with the wisdom of man, but as the Counselor comes, it will be revealed to us, and we will be able to understand (John 16:8; 1 Corinthians 2:13).

Some people say that Jesus is taking a rest by sitting at the right hand of the Father, following His death and the resurrection. But that is not what the Bible says: "The Lord said to my Lord: 'Sit at my right hand until I make your enemies a footstool for your feet'" Psalm 110:1, Acts 2:35). The Bible also says that when the enemies become a footstool for the feet of the Lord Jesus, it will be the time that Jesus comes again

(1 Corinthians 15:25). Therefore, He will continue with His salvation ministry until the day He returns.

There are some people who misunderstand the words of Jesus in John 19:30: "It is finished." They believe this to mean that Jesus has completed His ministry. But Jesus says that this means that He has completed His ministry here on Earth, for He has come in flesh. According to Revelation 21:6, Jesus' ministry will be completed when He declares, "It is done."

We have been made holy once for all through the sacrifice of the body of Jesus Christ (Hebrews 10:10). Jesus is sitting at the right hand of God; He has a permanent priesthood and is still judging righteously and working His ministry of salvation (Hebrews 7:24; Psalm 9:4).

> ✘ *Therefore he is able to save completely those who come to God through him, because he always lives to* **intercede** *for them.*
>
> *Hebrews 7:25*

> ✘ *Christ Jesus…is at the right hand of God and is also* **interceding** *for us.*
>
> *Romans 8:34*

> ✘ *We have* **one who speaks to the Father** *in our defense—Jesus Christ, the Righteous One.*
>
> *I John 2:1*

The Bible says that Jesus has gone through the heavens to the Father and is still interceding for us; this means that He is still working His ministry of salvation. So, when Jesus says, "that the Counselor will convict the world," He means

"I will go to the Father and become the high priest for you so that you can be justified" (John 16:10).

> ✍ *Every high priest is selected from among **men** and is appointed to represent them in matters related to God, to offer gifts and sacrifices for sins*
> *Hebrews 5:1*

There was a condition that every high priest had to be selected from among men, and that is why Jesus came in the flesh to us and rose again from the dead, in the flesh. He was delivered over to death for our sins and was raised to life for our justification (Romans 4:25; John 16:10). Some people say that we only have to believe in the resurrection of Christ, but the Bible says that we must also believe that He went to the Father. In being our high priest, He is bringing the atonement offering for us. And this is what we have to hold firmly to in our faith (Hebrews 4:14).

Leviticus 16 explains the atonement day. There were three conditions that had to be satisfied in order to bring the atonement offering (sin offering).

1. There had to be a high priest.
2. There had to be an altar
3. There had to be an offering

Before the Israelites made the tabernacle at the Mount Sinai, God called Moses to come up to the mountain and showed Moses the pattern of the tabernacle (Exodus 25:9), telling him to make the tabernacle and all its furnishings exactly like this pattern (Exodus 25:9, 40, 26:30, 27:8).

> ✍ *They serve at a sanctuary that is a copy and shadow of what is in heaven. This is why Moses was warned*

> when he was about to build **the tabernacle:** "See to
> it that you make everything according to the pattern
> shown you on the mountain."
>
> *Hebrews 8:5*

Here, the Bible says God showed Moses a pattern; this means that there is a true temple in heaven (Revelation 11:19 – in Revelation, the temple in heaven is mentioned about ten times between chapters 14 and 16). But even this temple in heaven will not be needed when "it is done": the saving ministry of Jesus and God, the Father almighty, and the Lamb, Jesus, will be its temple (Revelation 21:22).

The temple—the true tabernacle of God in heaven—is not something that's made by man, but is set up by the Lord (Hebrews 8:2).

> ⚸ *When Christ came as **high priest** of the good things
> that are already here, he went through the greater
> and **more perfect tabernacle** that is not man-
> made, that is to say, not a part of this creation. He
> did not enter by means of the blood of goats and
> calves: but he entered the Most Holy Place once
> for all **by his own blood**, having obtained eternal
> redemption.*
>
> *Hebrews 9:11-12*

Jesus rose again from the dead, went to the Father through the heavens, and became our high priest. And with His blood (instead of blood of animals) as a sin offering , He has offered for all time one sacrifice for our sins to the Father in the true tabernacle of heaven. He did not enter a man-made sanctuary that was only a copy of the true one; He entered heaven itself (John 16:10), now to appear for us in God's presence (Hebrews 9:24, 10:12; Romans 8:34; Ephesians 1:20).

> ✙ *But when this priest had offered for all time **one sacrifice for sins**, he sat down at the right hand of God.*
>
> *Hebrews 10:12*

> ✙ *Because by one sacrifice he **has made perfect forever** those who are being made holy.*
>
> *Hebrews 10:14*

We generally say that our sins were washed on the cross. But to be exact, our sins were washed by the resurrection of Christ, because He went to the Father, and because He offered for all time one sacrifice for sins with His blood.

> ✙ *Christ is the end of the law so that there may be righteousness for everyone who believes.*
>
> *Romans 10:4*

The most important thing in the laws of the Old Testament is offering a sacrifice. For Jesus to be the end of the law, He had to complete the most important thing from the law: offering a sacrifice. And Jesus became the end of the law by bringing the ultimate sacrifice of His blood to the living Father in the true tabernacle of God.

Therefore, Paul says in 1 Corinthians 15:17, "And if Christ has not been raised, your faith is futile: you are still in your sins," Because without the resurrection of Christ, Jesus wouldn't have become the end of the law. He had to become the end of the law (Romans 4:25) for our justification because He could not have become the end of the law unless He made the sacrifice for sins in heaven. Jesus made the sacrifice for all, and that is why the book of Hebrews says the following:

> ✘ *Then he adds: "Their sins and **lawless acts** I will remember no more."*
>
> *Hebrews 10:17*

Jesus became the high priest for us. He made the sacrifice for our sins with His blood so that the sin and lawless acts of all men who believe in Him would not be remembered by God.

The Old Testament is the shadow of the New Testament. It is the prophecy and written records about Christ Jesus (Luke 24:44; John 5:39). The offerings from the Old Testament are only a shadow of the offering that Jesus brought to the Father in heaven with His blood, but they are not the realities themselves (Hebrews 10:1).

Leviticus 16 shows us that God has set the date for atonement: on the tenth day of the seventh month, people had to deny themselves and not do any work because on this day, atonement was made for them, to cleanse them. This day was a good model and a shadow of the salvific ministry of Jesus Christ (Hebrews 10:1). Now, I will compare the works of a priest on the Day of Atonement in Leviticus 16 and the salvific ministry of Jesus as high priest.

1. On the Day of Atonement, the priest had to bathe himself with water before he put on the sacred garments (Leviticus 16: 4). Jesus washed Himself in the water of the Jordan River to start His salvific ministry. (Matthew3:16)
2. The priest put on the sacred garments (Leviticus 16:4). Jesus was dressed in a gorgeous purple robe (Luke 23:11).

3. The priest put on a linen turban (Leviticus 16:4). A twisted crown of thorns was set on Jesus' head (Mark 15:17).

4. The priest was to put incense on the fire before the Lord, and the smoke of the incense concealed the atonement cover the mercy seat above the testimony (Leviticus 16:13). According to Revelation 5:8, the incense is the prayers of the saints, and Jesus prayed earnestly until his sweat was like drops of blood falling to the ground. Jesus put the incense on the fire before the Lord through His prayers (Luke 22:44).

5. The priest was to slaughter animals for his own sin offering (Leviticus 16:11, 15). Jesus died on the cross and shed His own blood (John 19:34).

6. The priest took the blood of the animals behind the curtain, the Most Holy Place, and sprinkled the blood on the atonement cover and in front of it (Leviticus 16:15). Being the high priest for us, Jesus entered the Most Holy Place once for all by His own blood, having obtained eternal redemption (Hebrews 9:12; Revelation 9:13).

7. A scapegoat (Azazel) carried on itself all the sins of the Israelites to a solitary place and was released in the desert (Leviticus 16:22). All the disciples (Matthew 26:56), the governor's soldiers (Matthew 27:30), people who passed by (Matthew 27:39), the chief priests, the teacher of the law, the elders (Matthew 27:41), the robbers who were crucified with Jesus (Matthew 27:44), nature (Matthew 27:45), and even God (Matthew 27:46) deserted and forsook Jesus.

8. After the blood of the animals for the sin offerings was brought into the Most Holy Place to make atonement, they were taken outside the camp. Their hides, flesh, and

offal were to be burned up (Leviticus 16:27, 4:12: Hebrews 13:11). Jesus also suffered outside the city gate to make the people holy through his own blood (Hebrews 13:12).

9. The priest lifted his hands toward the people and blessed them sacrificing the offerings (Leviticus 9:22). At the end of this world, Jesus will come back and take us to be with Him, that we may also be in heaven where He is (John 14:3, Revelation 1:7).

From all these examples, we see that the death of Christ (parallel to sacrificing an animal in the Old Testament) is not the only significant thing about the sacrifice that He has brought to the Father for us. The resurrection, His ascension to heaven, the sin offering of His blood in heaven, and His second coming are all important as well. But the cross is what shows us the love and righteousness of God most clearly, and it is the cross where Jesus shed all His blood. This was essential for His salvific ministry; therefore, we say that our sins were forgiven on the cross.

Now a question might arise here as to whether Jesus sacrificed the perfect offering for us in heaven. The Bible gives us the answer. In the Old Testament, the Bible says that fire came down from heaven several times as they brought the offering to God (all these offerings were shadows of the Jesus' true offering to God in heaven).

1. After Moses set up the tabernacle and sacrificed the very first offering to God, fire came out from the presence of the Lord (Leviticus 9:24).

2. As Solomon sacrificed the first offering to God after he built the temple for the Lord, fire came down from heaven (2 Chronicles 7:1).

3. As King David built an altar to the Lord at the threshing floor of Araunah, the Jebusite, and sacrificed offerings, fire came down from heaven (1 Chronicles 21:26).
4. As Elijah sacrificed offerings on Mount Carmel, fire from the Lord fell from heaven (1 Kings 18:38).

Fire came down as evidence that Jesus sacrificed a perfect offering for us when people gathered on the day of Pentecost (Acts 2:3). That the Spirit of God came from heaven in the form of fire is evidence that Jesus sacrificed the perfect offering for us.

> *They saw what seemed to be tongues of fire that separated and came to rest on each of them.*
>
> *Acts 2:3*

God completed the way for people who believe in Jesus to have forgiveness. They, the sinners, have to know it and believe that Jesus is their Lord and Savior. The following are things that will happen to those who believe in Jesus.

- They will receive forgiveness.
- They will be reborn and become a new creature.
- They will have salvation.
- They will receive the Spirit of God.
- They will be justified.
- They will be called children of God.
- They will have eternal life.
- They will be citizens of the Kingdom of God.
- Their inheritance will be in heaven.
- They will live with God forever and ever.

CHAPTER 4

BY BELIEVING IN JESUS CHRIST AND CONFESSING THAT HE IS OUR LORD AND SAVIOR, WE WILL BE SAVED.

Believe in the Lord Jesus, and you will be
saved—you and your household.
Acts 16:31

By believing in the three things we have talked about, the faith in your heart, and by confessing with your mouth that Jesus is the Lord and Savior, you will be saved. This is a promise made by God.

Do you
1. confess that Jesus is the Son of God, your Lord and Savior?
2. believe in redemption through the cross?
3. believe in the resurrection of Christ Jesus?

If you not only know these three things but are also able to believe and confess with your mouth, then you are saved and a child of God. Hallelujah!! Congratulations! These are promises that the faithful God promised in Jesus Christ, by the Spirit.

The Bible says that we should repent and believe in Jesus. This means that we have to repent of our sins of leaving God and living as we saw it fit. We should turn our ways to God, put our faith in the Lord Jesus, and live according to His will (Acts 26:20).

But most of us do not even know whether we are saved or have any feelings. Some may feel sure that they are saved (Acts 9:4), but most people do not know. Jesus told Nicodemus that we are saved (John 3:16), that we have everlasting life, and that we are born again (John 3:3). Being "born again" means that we are born again spiritually, or that we are born by the Spirit of God. These three expressions are different, but they have the same meaning. When you are born again, you have everlasting life and are saved.

When we are born again, we are like newborn babies spiritually; so just like newborn babies, we do not know anything. We are spiritual newborn babies, and it is natural that we do not know whether or not we are saved and children of God. We are just born.

And just like newborn babies have to grow by being nursed, we have to be nursed; the Word of God is the pure, spiritual milk we need to be fed. We will grow by it in our salvation.

> ⍥ *Like newborn babies, crave pure **spiritual milk**, so that by it you may grow up in your salvation.*
> *1 Peter 2:2*

Like newborn babies naturally crave their mothers' milk, we, as newborn Christians, have to crave pure spiritual milk as well. Like a newborn baby crying out for his mother's milk, a saved, spiritual newborn baby has to cry out for the Word of God. It is just amazing how many people among *us* haven't grown up because they did not crave pure, spiritual milk and eat (1 Corinthians 3:1; Hebrews 5:13).

Like a newborn baby lives on milk and eats solid food as he grows, a spiritually newborn baby must live on the Word of God. And as we grow, we will learn more about spiritual things.

We especially have to pay attention to the part of the verse that says, "so that by it you may grow up in your salvation." Because the salvation that we have is the beginning, not the end; like a newborn baby has to grow up to be a man, we have to grow as well.

There are some who would say that there is no need for repentance or spiritual growth, since we are saved by faith in Jesus Christ. These people think that they can enter the kingdom of God just by believing in Christ Jesus. And to support their assertion, they hold up Luke 23:43 as an example: that the thief who was crucified with Jesus was saved. Of course, this is true. But then how should we interpret, "so that by it you may grow up in your salvation" (1 Peter 2:2) and "continue to work out your salvation with fear and trembling" (Philippians 2:12)?

Generally, the "salvation" discussed in the Bible is explained in three steps in theological terms.

The first step is *justification*, which means that you are saved by faith in Jesus Christ. God calls those who believe in Jesus Christ righteous, and they are spiritually reborn .

The next step is **sanctification**, meaning that we live as imitations of Christ. Our lives have to continue to changing and being transformed while we are in this world.

The final step is **glorification.** All believers and followers of the Christ will achieve eternal glory with Jesus Christ (Romans 8:18; 2 Corinthians 4:17).

Therefore, we have to continue to grow up in our salvation (Philippians 2:12). In order to do so, we must listen to the Word of God, read the Bible, study the Bible, memorize Scripture, and meditate on it, so that we may be able to apply the Word of God to our lives and grow up spiritually.

Some people say that it is really difficult to understand the Bible. But think about a newborn infant: newborns do not calculate or research their nutrition, but they live on milk and grow up. It is the same with us; we have to read the Word of God even if it is hard for us to understand. Then, we will grow up on it. As we grow up, we will understand the Bible more easily. So from which book of the Bible should we start? Billy Graham suggested reading from John. David Cho suggests reading from Mark. Both of these suggestions are good, but I would recommend reading the book of John again and again until you realize and understand who Jesus is. As you grow up spiritually, the Spirit of God will teach you and testify that you are saved.

> ✒ **The Spirit** himself testifies with our spirit that we are God's children.
>
> Romans 8:16

It can happen while you worship the Lord, read the Bible, pray, or drive: you will come to know that you are saved and have assurance in that. The Word of God says that the Spirit himself will testify this with our spirit. But remember that you are not saved when you have this realization, but from the moment that you put your faith in Jesus and confess Him as your Lord and Savior. This is the day that you are saved, and as you grow up spiritually, the Spirit of God will testify with your spirit.

There are people who have faith in Jesus Christ and are saved by their faith, yet they have not experienced how the Spirit of God testifies with their spirit. They doubt and ask themselves often whether or not they are really saved. Even without this experience, if you believe in Jesus, confess that He is your Lord and Savior, and live as an imitation of Christ, then you have salvation.

On the other hand, even when a person says that he or she is saved, if they do not have any changes or transformations in their life or are not obedient to God, they need to examine themselves (2 Corinthians 13:5).

As an infant grows up, he will learn more about his parents. In the same way, as we grow up spiritually, we will learn more about God and understand more about Jesus and His love (John 17:3).

- When you have salvation, your purpose in life will be changed (Isaiah 43:7; 1 Corinthians 10:31).
- When you have salvation, your life values will be changed (Philippians 3:7-9; Hebrews 11:24-26).
- When you have salvation, your priorities in life will be changed (Matthew 6:33, 10:37).

By examining yourself, your purpose in life, your values, and your priorities, you can test your salvation.

CHAPTER 5

THE THREE WAYS TO HAVE SALVATION, ACCORDING TO THE BIBLE.

The Bible records three ways to have our sins forgiven and to have salvation.

1. By believing in the Gospel (Romans 1:16)
2. By believing in Jesus Christ (Romans 10:9)
3. By calling on the name of the Lord (Romans 10:3) 13

All above three sound different, but mean the same thing. Believing in the Gospel and believing in Jesus Christ are the same, and so is calling on the name of the Lord.

The apostle Peter (Acts 2:36) and the apostle Paul (Romans 1:4) called Jesus "the Lord and Christ." The apostle John called Jesus "the Son of God and Christ" (John 20:31). And all three said the same thing about faith throughout the Bible.

The Lord (the Son of God)	Jesus	Christ
(The Divinity of God)	(Human Nature)	(The Death and the Resurrection)
Personality		Ministry (Work)

When we say that we believe in Jesus, we are actually saying that He is God, that He came to us in human nature, and that He is the Lord and Savior. Believing in Jesus

Christ is believing what He has done to save sinners—that He died and rose again for our sins.

Romans gives a good account of how a sinner gets saved and becomes righteous by having his sins washed away. The introduction of Romans records the content of the Gospel (Romans 1:3-4) and says the name of Christ Jesus.

✘ *Regarding his Son, who as to his human nature was a descendant of David, and who through the Spirit of holiness was declared with power to be the Son of God by his resurrection from the dead: Jesus Christ our Lord.*

Romans 1:3-4

"...his human nature was a descendant of David" (Romans 1:3) explains something about the human nature of Jesus. "...through the Spirit of holiness was declared with power to be the Son of God" (Romans 1:4) explains the divinity of Jesus Christ: Jesus is God, who came to us in human nature. He died and rose again from the dead for us. This is displayed in the diagram below:

The Son of God + Jesus + The Death and the Resurrection
(Romans 1:4)   (Romans 1:3)   (Romans 1:4)

These are the perfect contents of the Gospel. The apostle Paul regards the contents of the Gospel as the Lord / Jesus / Christ (Romans 1:4). This is the perfect name of Jesus.

The Lord + Jesus + Christ + The Death and the Resurrection (Romans 10:9)

These are the perfect contents included in believing in Jesus Christ. Finally, we can recognize that, as it is written in Romans 10:9, salvation by believing in Jesus, the core contents of the Gospel, and the salvific meaning of the name of the Lord Jesus Christ all have the same meaning.

At this point, I would like to compare what Peter, John and Paul wrote about salvation.

- By believing in Jesus, you will be saved (Romans 10:9). – Paul
- By believing in the Gospel (Romans 1:5), you will belong to Jesus Christ (Romans 1:6). – Paul
- By believing that Jesus is the Son of God, you will have eternal life (John 20:31). – John
- By believing that Jesus is your Lord and Savior (Acts 2:36), you will receive the gift of the Holy Spirit (Acts 2:38). – Peter

Through these examples, we can see that John, Peter, and Paul are all saying the same things about salvation and how to be saved. We can also see these things in what the angel said to the shepherds on the night Jesus was born: "Do not be afraid. I bring you good news [the Gospel] of great joy that will be for all the people. Today in the town of David a Savior has been born to you [Human Nature]: he is Christ [Ministry] the Lord [Divine Nature]" (Luke 2:10-11). We can confirm that all methods of gaining salvation in the New Testament have the same contents in these three expressions: "a Savior has been born in the town of David" (Human Nature), "the Lord" (Divine Nature), and "Christ" (Ministry).

Therefore, this is the main point, the foundation of faith, and the core of the Bible. It is the Gospel, the contents of faith, and the meaning of the name of the Lord. But unfortunately, many Christians have neglected the Bible's main point.

Chuck Colson, the founder of Prison Fellowship, once said, "Many American Christians do not know Christianity well."

What about Korean Christians? I have met a lot of people who planned to be pastors and ministers, but even they did not know this truth—the basis of Christianity. There have even been people who pretended to know it well. But the truth is that not many people know and understand this truth.

Romans 1:8 says, "Your faith is being reported all over the world." The faith of the Christians in Rome was being reported all over the world. They were mature Christians who obeyed the Word of God, as it is written in Romans 16:19: "Everyone has heard about your obedience." But to these people, the apostle Paul wrote in Romans 1:15, "That is why I am so eager to preach the Gospel also to you who are at Rome."

Why did he say that? It was because the Christians in Rome did not know the Gospel and how to believe in Jesus.

We cannot be rooted in Jesus Christ unless we know and understand this basic and most important core of the Gospel (Colossians 2:7). Without being rooted in this, we might be shaken when the time of trouble comes. So not only the Roman Christians of Paul's time, but we also should know this (1 Peter 3:15).

Even in Old Testament times, people could be saved by believing in the nature of and works of God (Exodus 20:2; Leviticus 11:45, 19:36, 22:33, 26:13; Numbers 15:41; Deuteronomy 5:5; Psalms 81:10; Hosea 13:4):

> ✘ *I am the Lord your God, who brought you out of Egypt, out of the land of slavery.*
>
> *Exodus 20:2*

I could rewrite this verse as,

> The nature of God: I am the Lord your God.
> The works of God: I brought you out of Egypt, out the land of slavery.

The Old Testament is the prophecy and Shadow of the New Testament. Therefore, it can be said that the salvation of the Israelites from their slavery in Egypt is a shadow of the salvation of those who were once slaves of sin, but now believe in Jesus Christ. So the Lord's promise to save those who believed in the Lord and what He had done in the Old Testament is the same as the truth revealed in the New Testament: that we will be forgiven and saved if we believe in Jesus Christ and confess that He is our Lord and Savior.

One thing that we have to consider is that the Psalms are actually songs and prayers to God. The Psalms tell us two reasons why we should praise the Lord and pray to Him:

1. We should praise the Lord, for He is our God and He is good.

2. We should praise the Lord for what He has done for us

Isaiah, the book from the Old Testament that is also called the "evangelical prophet" because it prophesied the most about the Messiah, mentions the human nature of the Christ (Isaiah 9:6) and the ministry of the Christ (Isaiah 53:4-6) many times. It is also the same as the Gospel.

The reason the Israelites had to live in vain in the time of Judges is recorded in Judges 21:25: "In those days Israel had no king: everyone did as he saw fit." Their king was God, but they did not know this, which is why they sought a king. Why did they do this? According to the Bible, this is why:

> *After that whole generation had been gathered to their fathers, another generation grew up, who knew* **neither the Lord nor what he had done** *for Israel.*
> *Judges 2:10*

The first generation died, and the next generation did not know

1. who God is
2. what He had done for Israel

So they served idols, like Baal, and various gods of the people around them.

> *Then the Israelites did evil in the eyes of the Lord and served the Baal. They forsook the Lord, the God of their fathers, who had brought them out of Egypt. They followed and worshipped various gods of the*

> *peoples around them. They provoked the Lord to*
> *anger.*
>
> *Judges 2:11-12*

The Bible shows us the result of the Israelites' idol worship because the Israelites did not know who God is or what He had done for them:

> ✘ *Whenever Israel went out to fight, the hand of the Lord was against them to defeat them, just as he had sworn to them. They were in great distress.*
>
> *Judges 2:15*

Just as faith and salvation are the contents of the Gospel in the New Testament (Romans 10:9), the Israelites should have known who God is and what He had done for them. But they knew neither God's identity nor God's works for them. So they served idols and the Baals. If we do not learn to know God, believe what the Lord has done for us, and make Him the center of our lives, the same thing will happen to us; we will serve idols like money, self, reputation, pleasure, and evil things. Just like the Israelites in the time of Judges, we will live in vain.

People who do not know God and what He has done for them live in vain. Because of their lack of knowledge, they serve idols, such as materialism. The Baals were the gods of materialism. People who served the Baals lived in vain, and so do the people who follow materialism now. Their life is not easy, but it is in vain; many of them attempt suicide.

This 21st century we are living in is the time of vanity— without the truth, but with people who doing as they see fit. It's an inevitable consequence of not knowing Jesus and what He has done for us. Mammonism and materialism are prevalent nowadays. But like the Israelites who served the Baals, Mammonism and materialism will fail.

Deuteronomy 1:2 says that it took eleven days to go from Horeb to Kadesh Barnea. It's actually just about 165 miles (264 kilometers). Moses recorded in Deuteronomy 2:14 that it took 38 years for the Israelites to get from Kadesh Barnea across the Zered Valley. It's actually just 81 miles (130 kilometers) between these two places. It should have taken them 6 days at most, but it took them 38 years. And still they were not able to cross, so that 600,000 fighting men died in the desert. Only three people from the first generation crossed the Zered Valley: Moses, Joshua, and Caleb.

The first and second books of Timothy are the letters that the apostle Paul sent to Timothy to teach him how to do ministry. Timothy spent almost 20 years with Paul in the mission field, so he must have learned a lot from Paul. Timothy was already a minister, but as Paul wrote to Timothy, he mentioned the Gospel many times (1 Timothy 1:12, 3:16; 2 Timothy 1:10, 2:8). This shows us how important the foundation of faith is.

Therefore, we have to teach the Gospel to Christians. Like the Israelites who had to wander in the desert for 38 year (a journey that could have taken only 6 days), there are people who do not come to know and understand the Gospel, even though they have been going to church for a very long time. This is so sad.

> ✒ ...that God was reconciling the world to himself in Christ, not counting men's sins against them. And he **has committed** to us the message of reconciliation.... Be reconciled to God. God made him who had no sin

> *to be sin for us, so that in him we might become the*
> *righteousness of God.*
>
> *2 Corinthians 5:19-21*

Whoever believes in Jesus will have his sin removed by God and placed on Jesus, and the righteousness of Christ Jesus, instead of sin, will clothe him. So whoever believes will be righteous. God has promised us that whoever believes in Jesus will be forgiven and saved. If you believe in this promise and in Christ Jesus, you will be clothed with the righteousness of Jesus, and you will be saved. Amen.

CONCLUSION

At the beginning of this book, I asked you three important questions about your life:

1. **Where do I come from?**
2. **Why do I live in this world?**
3. **Where am I really heading to?**

The answers to these questions cannot be found by philosophers, but those who believe in Jesus Christ will be able to answer these questions with confidence.

- The answer to the first question is, **"I come from the Lord."**
- The answer to the second question is, **"I have found the way to the Lord."**
- The answer to the third question is, **"I am heading to my Lord."**

It is such a blessing to be a child of God. It is a grace from the Lord to have salvation. From now on, we should be sanctified and holy in all we do (1 Thessalonians 4:3; 1 Peter

1:15), following the likeness of Jesus Christ (Romans 8:29; 2 Corinthians 3:18). To be a Christian means to be a follower of Christ, or to belong to Christ. In order to belong to Christ and be a follower of Him, we have take Christ into the center of our hearts and have the same attitude as that of Christ Jesus (Matthew 11:29; Philippians 2:5). We have to be His; ones who belong to Christ are true Christians.

Dear Lord, let all Your children know who You are, believe in You, and love You more. Amen.